BUILD YOUR PLAYBOOK FOR MANAGING SUPPLY CHAIN TRANSACTIONS

WITH DESKTOP TOOLS, REFERENCES AND SAMPLE FORMS

FIRST EDITION

X. Paul Humbert Esq.
Robert C. Mastice MSNE

Foreword by: Professor Darren J. Prokop

Who Should Use this Book? Anyone involved in studying, developing, managing or implementing supply / demand chains, projects, purchases or any complex transaction or procurement where cost, schedule and scope certainty are important. This includes Students, Project Managers, Supply / Demand Chain Management Professionals, Risk Managers, Insurance Experts, Purchasing Agents, Buyers, Category Managers, Auditors, Attorneys, Contract Administrators, CFOs / CPOs, Executives, as well as change management, transformation and integration experts.

What Will This Book Do for You? *PLAYBOOK* provides a clear and well defined process for building or improving your supply chain transaction process. The book blends the practical with best practices for the management of transactions from cradle-to-grave. There is often a gap between the theory of supply chain management and its actual practice. *PLAYBOOK* bridges that gap and provides a methodology for applying best practices tailored to the individual organization's unique needs.

Note: The information provided in this book covers concepts and principles that have stood the test of time. However, all transactions are fact specific and case sensitive. Your organization may have special needs or unique requirements. This text is not intended to provide legal advice or guidance regarding specific transactions. Consult your subject matter experts.

OTHER BOOKS BY THE AUTHORS

Contract and Risk Management for Supply Chain Management Professionals, ISBN: 10:0615956718; ISBN 13:9780615956718; Library of Congress Control No: 2014901576, available through Amazon.com.

Model Contract Terms and Conditions with Annotations and Case Summaries, ISBN 10: 0692272089; ISBN 13:9780692272084; Library of Congress Control No: 2014914436, available through Amazon.com.

Printed in the United States of America | Library of Congress Cataloging-in-publication
ISBN-13: 9780692412947
ISBN-10: 0692412948

Library of Congress Control Number: 2015904884
X. Paul Humbert, Summit, NJ

TABLE OF CONTENTS

LIST OF SAMPLE DESKTOPS AND TOOLS

PREFACE

"It must be considered that there is nothing more difficult to carry out,
nor more doubtful of success, nor more dangerous to handle,
than to initiate a new order of things."

Niccolo Machiavelli, 1469-1527

Although everyone appreciates the theoretical need for change, most people fear and resist it to the end. Too much change at a faster pace than people can assimilate can be problematic. The best path to successful change may be a process of improvement rather than something more draconian. After all, Machiavelli also said:

"He who desires or attempts to reform…and wishes to have it accepted, must at least retain the semblance of old forms; so that it may seem to the people that there has been no change in the institutions."

FOREWORD
By Professor Darren J. Prokop

PLAYBOOK provides a detailed look at how to construct a set of critical documents for organizations connected in supply and demand chains. Humbert and Mastice carefully walk you through the logistics and show you how to handle the legalese using wisdom and some pithy remarks along the way. To add a favorite of my own, W. Edwards Deming, the great management thinker, was famous for saying: "If you can't describe what you're doing as a process, you don't know what you're doing." Humbert and Mastice give you a process...in 49 steps.

While the suggested pathway in *PLAYBOOK* is common to most supply and demand chains, those who use it will see the value in adapting it to their specific business requirements. This is where the art of relationship management comes in. Of course, relationship management is enhanced when each side has command of the facts. In order to make sure your organization is ready for the 49 step process, Humbert and Mastice suggest 19 internal documents necessary to make sure your team is in line and contingencies (e.g., financial risk) are accounted for. Indeed, we should not fear risk...for that is the price in any business relationship...but learn how to control it.

PLAYBOOK, as a title, invokes a sports analogy. Like all sports, it is maneuverability which takes a team to the finish line. Movement and flexibility are fundamental attributes in supply and demand chain management to-day. This is because any "solution" to the problem of pricing, costing, lo-gistics network design, etc. is only valid until the business environment changes. And change is always occurring because that is the nature of hu-man beings in a free market. With a process in place, an organization can afford to be proactive and not merely reactive. But, is there no constant amid this sea of change? Yes there is. Humbert and Mastice, as experts, note that contract law is virtually unchanging; and whatever part of it may be subject to fluctuation (e.g., the concept of "good faith") serves to remind us that relationship management is still important. A good contract is pre-pared bilaterally and yet, often times, one party simply agrees to the terms put forward by the other party without careful negotiation. For example, small shippers typically accept a transportation carrier's contract of car-riage (which can be a formidable document) without too much discussion of contingency on their side. This is unfortunate because it demonstrates a lack of process. Still, contracts are never perfect and the parties within them need to be nurtured for as long as their relationship exists.

Humbert and Mastice understand that supply and demand chains are not just linkages through which inputs and finished goods move to their ulti-mate customer; rather, they are a means by which people meet, negotiate, and contract with each other. The human factor...in the form of relation-ship management...is often underappreciated in our field. *PLAYBOOK* reminds us that "a good beginning makes for a good ending." Begin your foray into the practice of supply and demand chain management with this well-written book.

Dr. Darren Prokop
Professor of Logistics
College of Business and Public Policy
University of Alaska Anchorage

The College of Business and Public Policy at the University of Alaska Anchorage offers undergraduate and graduate degrees in logistics and supply chain management. These degrees were constructed, in collaboration with industry, to meet the real-life needs of domestic and international businesses. Alaska, at the global crossroad, is a gateway for U.S.-Asia trade and transportation.

Dr. Darren Prokop has published seminal research in leading academic journals on a wide range of topics, including: the microfoundations of logistics; air cargo logistics; cabotage regulations; and supply chain security modelling. He has written, and contributed chapters to, several books in the field.

AUTHORS' NOTES

Just as most individuals believe they understand others and the world better than they actually do, most business professionals understand supply and demand chain transactions less well than they think.

This "illusion of knowledge" has its basis in not only general overconfidence about one's experience, knowledge and expertise, but in the tendency of people to draw conclusions based on what they want to believe. People also tend to take mental shortcuts in making assumptions and decisions that may or may not be accurate. There are, of course, also the proverbial "unknown, unknowns", i.e. the things we don't know, we don't know. *PLAYBOOK* encourages readers to think / re-think about the supply and demand chain process, challenge what is currently being done within their organization, identify what could be done better (or what is being done that is unnecessary / counterproductive) and take appropriate action to improve and implement the optimal process.

PLAYBOOK enlightens the reader by outlining and detailing the supply chain transaction process steps around which that organization can model or modify its own processes. Understanding and adapting the steps *PLAYBOOK* offers yields a pathway for an organization to build its own playbook, uniquely designed but built on sound practices. Moreover,

PLAYBOOK offers the opportunity to position an organization to promote consistency, ensure efficiency, avoid risk and create opportunities in today's highly competitive, ever changing global supply chain management industry. Once an organization institutes a playbook it cannot only adjust to change but also anticipate and adapt to change to avoid or at least minimize what all executives, as well as large and small business alike, fear most…RISK.

You may ask: "How can an organization balance consistency and predictability in its supply chain transactions with continuous improvement?" The answer is that without a consistent and predictable track record it may not be possible to determine how to make improvements. *PLAYBOOK* helps to ensure that transformation, integration and continuous improvement are part of an organization's playbook by having a clear process for recording lessons learned and continuously implementing process improvement.

Each organization should develop its own unique playbook taking into consideration its existing capabilities, systems, personnel, needs and requirements. The secret is to follow a disciplined process and protocol for achieving an optimal playbook. *PLAYBOOK* does that for you and ensures that you will follow a predicable path toward achieving the right balance between a highly structured approach and the flexibility necessary to accomplish your organization's goals. Note that efficient and effective consistency, not perfection, is the goal. However, "Nothing succeeds like excess" as the saying goes.

The greatest risk to a sound process is individuals, either well-meaning or ignorant, deviating from an organization's best interests by doing things "their way". The problem manifests itself in several ways. Often, long service employees may have "one year's experience 30 times", or they may have been doing the "wrong thing" for so long that it has become an unchallenged practice. As noted, many people are simply blind to the risk that "they don't know what they don't know."

In addition, the legacy of doing the wrong thing for so many years is that individuals and even organizations are reluctant to change patterns even though they cannot remember, let alone articulate a rationale for, why they do something a certain way. Many times procedures are followed, data collected and actions are taken that have no use, positive affect or purpose other than honoring misguided precedent. The discipline of going through *PLAYBOOK* prompts a fresh look and challenge to embedded procedures which may have become unnecessary, duplicative, sub-par or even harmful.

It is a fact that today's organizations are often made up of employees who have prior work experience in other organizations. The natural result is that these employees "impart" their former employer's way of doing things. This may or may not be a good way of doing things but certainly no good can come from everyone approaching the same tasks differently.

The power and efficiency of having the entire "team" acting in concert cannot be overstated. It is a huge advantage to any organization to have the focus of the effort be known and predictable to all parties in order to yield a consistent and high quality outcome time and time again. This is not to say that improvements cannot be made or that individual initiative should be stifled. Process improvement and lessons learned is part of the *PLAYBOOK* process and should be part of every organization. Mistakes and missed opportunities do occur and are part of the normal learning process. However, repeating the same mistakes over and over again is unacceptable. *PLAYBOOK* guards against that and provides a defined framework for process improvement instead of relying on vague (and difficult to implement) notions of "culture change".

Another challenge facing organizations is training. Training is both expensive and time consuming. There is also a very real question of how effective training actually is in changing behavior. It is far too easy to attend training sessions and walk away with no changes in behavior. A sound playbook mitigates that risk by providing the associate with not only a step-by-step process to follow, but the necessary desktop references and tools to utilize on a real-time basis. Thus, training efforts are reinforced. The desktop references and related tools may seem a bit aggressive but every single right and remedy outlined is not necessarily "a hill to die for" as the saying goes. It's best to start out with ambitious positions and "aim high" in order to "finish high". Test the tools provided as you tailor the optimal playbook for your organization.

"Accountability" is a word often heard in organizations these days. All too often there is no real way to measure, let alone enforce, accountability. *PLAYBOOK* provides a clear and measurable "audit path" for accountability. If a step in the process is missed or a resource is not used, it becomes a matter of record and further instruction or appropriate corrective action is taken. Accountability is a basic building block of trust. Employees who see accountability applied know the organization is serious about good contract management.

Note that the perfect process and perfect tools have not yet been written. *PLAYBOOK* is no exception. However, *PLAYBOOK* provides a strong basis on which to initially craft and subsequently refine a definitive process. Internal and external subject matter experts, as well as legal advisors, further define and strengthen those fundamentals. This book provides a blueprint for structuring your playbook to its maximum advantage and "front loading the effort". Bear in mind that everything takes longer than you think. Building your playbook is no exception.

PLAYBOOK addresses numerous contracting pitfalls and provides lessons learned and guidance that are not typically taught at the college or even graduate school level. One of the key lessons is that no process or contract is "self-guiding" or "self-managing" but rather requires active and daily management and attention in order to fulfill its intended purpose. Moreover, it is easy to quickly lose, through poor administration or inadvertent waiver, hard won contract rights. Far too many contracts are simply "filed and forgotten" until problems erupt. Sometimes it is even a challenge to find a copy of the contract, let alone a signed version. Avoid the embarrassment of having to ask the other party for a copy of the contract. *PLAYBOOK* not only provides procedures and steps but also includes desktop references and tools providing sample guidance on the all-important post-execution contract management phase of the transaction. Use *PLAYBOOK* to create your own playbook, specific to your organization's needs.

ABOUT THE AUTHORS

X. Paul Humbert, Esq.

Paul Humbert is President of the Humbert Group, LLC, which provides consulting services with particular emphasis on complex negotiations, strategic alliances, process improvement, risk management techniques, project management assistance, training and coaching, as well as post-execution contract management including dispute resolution. Paul holds degrees in both business and law and has extensive experience in these areas. He is an expert in structuring agreements and contract management procedures that are clear and minimize the risk of claims or non-conforming deliverables.

In addition to assisting clients, Paul also teaches at the graduate school level. He is a lecturer at the Rutgers Business School – Newark and New Brunswick, NJ and has also served as Adjunct Professor at both Seton Law School and Monmouth College where he taught legal and business courses. Paul has also served as an arbiter for the American Arbitration Association. Paul is a frequent lecturer and guest speaker.

Contact Information: xphumbert@thehumbertgroup.net

Robert C. Mastice, MSME

Robert C. Mastice is Principal / Managing Director of Tri-Power Consulting Services, LLC ("Tri-Power"). Tri-Power provides services to fortune 500 companies in three areas: (a) project based contracting management / document management, (b) contingent labor contracting labor services for managed service programs (MSPs) and (c) business process modeling using custom built IT applications. Tri-Power's affiliate, Tri-Power Design, LLC provides electro-mechanical design, engineering, prototyping and manufacturing service to global companies for medical devices, consumer products as well as custom one-of-a-kind machine design, engineering and fabrication.

Robert has years of experience in contract creation, negotiation and management services. Robert has supported clients with contract terms and scope of work crafting, contract negotiations, and document management and control services as well as post-execution contract management. Robert holds advanced degrees in mechanical engineering and is an expert in managing the process of executing commercial transactions from "cradle-to-grave".

Contact Information: robert.mastice@tripower.net

INTRODUCTION

Contract, n. 1:
"An agreement between two or more parties
creating obligations that are enforceable by law."
- *Black's Law Dictionary*

Supply chain transactions cannot be managed without a basic understanding of the nature of contracts. The definition of a "contract" appears deceptively simple. This small group of words is simultaneously clear yet complex; obvious but nuanced. In fact, it is simply not possible to completely define the term "contract" in a sentence or two. Any short definition requires further explanation of the underlying principles and facts under which a contract can be created, changed or ended. Adding to the complexity is the fact that it can be very difficult to determine when negotiations have ended and a binding commitment (contract) entered into. It is crucial therefore to understand, and indeed very carefully control, the circumstances under which (as well as the moment when) the words or conduct demonstrate an intent to be legally bound, thereby creating a contract. We routinely enter into contracts, but rarely think through the process by which they are formed.

Perhaps a contract is best understood by how it is created. A contract occurs when an *offer* is *accepted,* supported by valuable *consideration*, for some *legal*

15

purpose, by *competent parties.* In a commercial context, these five elements presume the intent to be legally bound. Note that the test as to whether the parties intended to be legally bound is an "objective" one, i.e., what a reasonable person would determine based on the facts and circumstances, not some hidden "subjective" intent of either party. But not all promises create a contract. For example, social arrangements (e.g., "I will attend your wedding party") are usually not considered contractual in nature. Moreover, vagueness (or even incompleteness) does not necessarily preclude the creation of a contract. If parties agree on a quantity term and exhibit an intent to be bound based on the surrounding facts and circumstances, a contract is usually found to exist with all other terms and conditions capable of being determined by custom or law.

An "offer" occurs when something is presented for acceptance, e.g., a prospective purchaser issues a request for proposal (i.e., a request for an offer) and receives a proposal (i.e., an offer) in response. Offers can be accepted by words or conduct indicating that they are satisfactory. "Consideration" means anything of value such as money, a promise or even a promise not to do something (e.g. a release). Of course, you cannot contract for illegal purposes. The term "competent" in a contracting context doesn't mean smart or expert but simply "legally competent" to enter into an agreement and the threshold is low (e.g., individuals over 18 are typically "competent" to bind themselves legally).

The law facilitates the creation of contracts. Contracts are easy to enter into if the parties exhibit an objective intent to be bound and the elements of a contract are met (even if the details are vague or missing). But great care needs to be taken in controlling the moment when discussions or negotiations end and a commitment is created. This highlights the danger of oral agreements, letters of intent, memoranda of understanding and so-called "handshake" deals. If you are in the business of negotiating and managing contracts, you don't want the terms and conditions of your transaction to be supplied by a court or trade practice providing the missing details such as acceptable quality and reasonable delivery. Although vagueness does not preclude creating a contract, "agreements to agree" are unenforceable. This is why it is generally undesirable to rely on language such as "subject to mutual agreement" or "subject to equitable adjustment". A simple way of controlling the moment of contractual commitment is to make it clear from the very beginning that: "We have no deal unless and until a formal contract is duly executed by our authorized representatives", or words to that effect.

As complicated as defining what is meant by the word "contract", even more challenging is articulating what constitutes a "good" contract. Ideally, a contract is concise but also a complete articulation of each party's respective risks and responsibilities; clear despite its inherent complexity; and predictable while remaining flexible enough to accommodate change. Language itself provides the final challenge given its natural limitations. The perfect contract is yet to be written and "no matter how flat the pancake" there are always two sides. Against this backdrop, the additional challenge of managing the contract looms.

Contracts regulate every transaction we make, from buying a cup of coffee to consummating a merger or acquisition. Contracts have been with us a long time and are here to stay. But how well they are entered into and managed will increasingly be a competitive differentiator. Hence the need to manage the steps before, during and after a contract is entered into - in other words, from "cradle-to-grave".

The following basic principles governing contracts may put the complexities of supply chain transactions and the challenges of post-execution management in better perspective:

1. Words or conduct can create a contract or affect contract rights.

Usually, there is no legal requirement that a formal written contract be signed in order for a contract to exist. Verbal contracts, handshake deals or even conduct can create legally enforceable contractual commitments, however ill-advised. Accordingly, smart negotiators and contract managers not only control the moment of agreement but avoid inadvertently waiving contract rights or remedies. For example, as a buyer, suppose your contract gives you the right to insist on delivery by date certain (i.e., time is of the essence). If the seller contacts you to say that delivery will be late, your response might be, "Hurry up and deliver". If that happens, has a new contract been formed or the old contract modified? Much better and safer to reply, "You owed me delivery by date certain and failing to deliver on time is a breach. We are reserving all of our rights and remedies, including, but not limited to, the right to terminate the agreement or make a new date of the essence and to be made whole for any damages", or words to that effect. This is not being mean-spirited or unprofessional, but simply preserving your rights and remedies until you determine whether or how much you've been damaged by the breach.

2. Courts will generally not re-make a contract in your favor.

Contract liability and obligations are strict. Particularly, in the case of parties who are in the business of buying or selling goods or services (i.e., "merchants"), courts will strictly enforce the contracts between them, good or bad. Courts may come to the rescue of "widows and orphans", but will usually leave commercial entities with the deal they have made for themselves. Note also that courts are not in the business of determining that the "consideration" supporting the contract is fair or even adequate. Hence, contracts often recite "one dollar" in consideration.

3. The typical remedy for breach is money (damages), not punishment.

With few exceptions, the usual remedy for breach of contract is monetary damages, i.e., financial compensation to make the injured party "whole" for the loss of the benefit of the bargain. For example, if you contract with someone to paint your house for $3,000 and they inexcusably don't perform the work at all, and you hire someone else to paint your house for $3,300, your damages are $300. By the same token, if the replacement contractor charges you $2,700, your compensatory damages are zero. This is a gross simplification and there may be other factors at play, but it illustrates the basic concept. Note that penalties are not recoverable for mere breach of contract. However, in some circumstances the parties can agree up front (stipulate) what the damages would be in the event of a breach. These are called liquidated damages. They are simply a reasonable estimate of the damages to be incurred as a result of a breach and are appropriate when calculating actual damages would be very difficult. Note that you should never refer to liquidated damages as "penalties" or "bonus-penalty" provisions. Not only are penalties unenforceable, but there is no logical or legal requirement that you have a bonus provision in a contract simply because you have liquidated damages. Liquidated damages are a remedy for breach. A bonus is something paid for extraordinary performance. You can have one without the other, both or neither.

4. The contract is only by and between the named parties.

Generally, only the actual parties (i.e., signatories) are bound by the terms of the contract; not for example subsidiaries or affiliates who may be "related" to one of the parties to the contract. Indeed, contractual liability, although strict, is by design limited liability. That is why entities often form special purpose legal entities with limited financial resources. Each such entity (e.g. a subsidiary, limited liability company, etc.) is its own legal "person". This is not illegal and allows risk to be "parked" with or placed upon an entity which may perhaps have limited resources. Of course, doing business with such an entity may increase the risk for the other party. Hence, the desire for financial guarantees from some third party in the form of, for example, parental guarantees or letters of credit.

5.   By your actions or inactions, you can create the power in others to contractually bind you even if they do not have the actual authority to do so.

When one party acts in such a manner as to cause another to reasonably believe that an individual has authority to contractually bind that party, and the other party reasonably relies on those acts to its detriment, something called "apparent authority" has been created. If you let your employees or representatives act as if they have authority, courts may well determine that your conduct has given them that authority regardless of what your internal protocols or bylaws say. Avoid the "apparent authority" trap by being clear with third parties as to who has actual authority to commit your organization. By the same token, understand who has the actual authority to contract and bind the counterparty with whom you are dealing.

6.   There is no automatic right to changing a contract.

If you want to have the right to change a contract, you must build change flexibility into it. Everything changes and this includes needs and circumstances. By building change capability into your contract you can address, as part of the original deal, how changes will be incorporated, including at what price or credit.

7.   Once you accept goods or services, you have fewer rights, remedies and leverage.

Just as one must carefully control the moment of agreement, one must carefully confirm that the goods or services delivered or performed are conforming to the contract prior to acceptance. This may involve inspection or testing and neither receipt nor payment necessarily constitute acceptance. Build an appropriate period or protocol for inspection or testing into your contracts and avoid an inadvertent acceptance. For example, if you are asked to sign a document upon delivery and it contains language to the effect that the goods or services have been accepted, qualify your signature with the words "confirming delivery only."

> 8.   By contract, you can specify that the written agreement contains the only and entire agreement between the parties.

It is common for a contract to contain an "entire agreement" or integration clause reciting that the written agreement is the only and entire agreement between the parties. This means that past communications are not part of the deal unless included or referenced in the written contract. Courts will enforce this, but will also permit communications not included in the written contract (Parol Evidence) to explain but not vary the terms of the deal. Make sure the person signing the contract understands the effect of the integration clause.

> 9.   Contracts are not forever; anticipate the end.

There are three common ways a contract can end, namely: (a) expiration (although some rights, like warranties, insurance, or indemnities, may continue beyond the contract's expiration date); (b) termination for convenience (which is a right you negotiate and put in the contract); and (c) termination for cause (i.e., a breach of contract). Breach occurs when a party, without the right to do so, fails to follow the contract e.g., fails to perform, refuses to perform or commits an "anticipatory" breach. Anticipatory breach occurs when a party, by words or conduct, indicates they will not perform.

The right to demand adequate assurance that the contractor intends to perform its obligations is an important right to include in your contracts. This concept is borrowed from the Uniform Commercial Code and not typically found in most transactions. The key is to have just cause to demand said assurance. It provides a means to declare the contractor to be in breach before actual performance is due under the contract. Of course, if the contractor comes out and tells you it will not perform, that is a breach unless non-performance is justified. The failure to provide adequate assurance of future performance is the other way a breach can occur before performance is actually due under the contract.

Of course, if a contract becomes impossible or illegal (not merely more difficult or expensive) to perform it may be set aside (i.e., voided), potentially excusing future performance. Likewise, contracts based on some sort of misrepresentation amounting to fraudulent inducement can result in the contract being set aside and damages recovered. In addition, a contract can be set aside in cases where both parties are under the same error regarding a fundamental fact. Errors of judgment are not "mistakes" in this context. Generally, a unilateral mistake (a mistake by one party) does not excuse performance unless the mistake was material (very serious), made despite the exercise of due care, the other party is not seriously harmed except for the loss of the bargain, and enforcement of the contract would be unconscionable.

These nine (9) principles are by no means a complete list and only begin to cover what should be considered when entering or managing supply chain transactions. The principles are a beginning to a more in depth understanding as set forth in *PLAYBOOK*.

THE PLAYBOOK METHODOLOGY

Today's organizations are charged with creating lean, flexible and competitive business models focusing on: (a) delivering sustainable cost improvement, (b) transforming business capabilities, (c) integrating diverse procurement organizations, and (d) accomplishing more, faster and with greater efficiency.

To achieve world class performance, commercial sophistication rooted in high tech tools and skill sets will be required. This includes a structured methodology for entering into and managing commercial transactions fostering quality and consistency.

Management is also being asked to do more with less. Nowhere is this more evident than in the area of human capital. There are three (3) aspects of this problem: (a) fewer employees but more work, (b) new employees with little experience, and (c) experienced employees with legacy experience.

As previously noted, employees may have one year's experience 30 times. In addition, training new or existing employees is expensive, time consuming and may not always be effective. The question then becomes…how to get consistent and correct execution with good results?

The answer is to adopt a playbook so that everyone in your organization follows a standardized and collaborative step-by-step contracting process which articulates each step necessary to enter into well-structured transactions and properly manage them. *PLAYBOOK* sets the path to that success.

The benefits of the *PLAYBOOK* approach is that it: (a) leverages existing resources, (b) allows less experienced professionals to stay on course, (c) keeps experienced professionals from deviating from standards, (d) identifies potential areas for improvements including deleting duplicative or unnecessary steps, highlighting potential gaps or weak points in the process, and (e) mitigates risk.

In a playbook, steps are linked to templates, desktop procedures, forms or checklists to ensure that the necessary tools are readily available.

Accordingly, your organization's version of *PLAYBOOK* sets the stage for success in that it:

1. Creates an effective means to incorporate both best practices and keep staffing levels lean;
2. Provides a clear process with tools and procedures to ensure consistency and uniformity;
3. Can be tailored to the specific needs of your organization, yet flexible and scalable as your needs change;
4. Avoids large bureaucracy with home office staff by providing a clear path coupled with the necessary technologies and techniques;
5. Provides a clear process and road map for creating sound work scopes;
6. Provides centralized storage, facilitating ease of retrieval and a sound audit trail;

7.   Is user friendly and accessible on your SharePoint or cloud-based application;

8.   Provides a clear process for addressing claims and warranty issues including standardized template letters;

9.   Addresses every aspect of your transactions;

10.   Links tools with output in an integrated process;

11.   Documents the process for assessing and identifying needs, suitable suppliers, sourcing strategies, risks, on-going performance and lessons learned;

12.   Mitigates risk and permits process improvement and workforce optimization.

A playbook promotes clear roles and responsibilities breaking down "the silos" that tend to arise in organizations without clear direction. In addition, with a structured process and procedure in place there is less opportunity for errors or abuses to occur. Thus, a playbook not only promotes efficiency by harmonizing cross-company work practices and improving communication, but also reduces the risk of inappropriate (or even fraudulent) transactions. Finally, a playbook does not depend on expensive "big buck / bang" technological solutions.

BEYOND MERE PROCESS

UNDERSTANDING THE DUTY OF GOOD FAITH

The basic principles and elements of contracts have not changed since pre-Biblical times. The Code of Hammurabi, dating back to 1754 BC and carved into 8' high stone, states that parties are free to contract as they wish and reflects recourse to, and respect for, written agreements. And the Code of Hammurabi's is not the earliest of such codes, simply the best organized and most well preserved.

The time honored and oft-cited case of <u>Hadley v. Baxendale</u>, 9 Ex. Ch. 341 (1854) is testament to the fact that contract law is consistent and its fundamental underlying principles almost never change. This old English case is still good law and frequently cited for the proposition that a party is liable for all the foreseeable consequences of a breach of contract, unless damages are disclaimed or limited by the contract. In the case of contracts, "old law is good law." This makes perfect sense since the purpose of a contract is to create certainty and predictability.

One notable exception to the consistency of contract law is the relatively recent imposition by statute (Uniform Commercial Code / EU Code) and / or the common law (courts) of the duty of good faith. Jurisdictions around the world have now come to embrace the concept that parties owe each other the duty of good faith in the performance of contractual responsibilities.

Moreover, the application of this duty has consistently increased. The principle is most broadly recognized in the United States but is also applied in Great Britain, Canada, Australia and most of the EU Member States.

This duty, present by operation of law in all contracts, imposes the rather vague notion of "good faith" on both parties. Despite its importance, the term is routinely used by those in the contract process with little or no real understanding of its true meaning and practical application. The elusive definition makes it difficult to ensure the duty of good faith is followed by mere process alone. Process, though crucial to success, will never eliminate the need to educate staff regarding the subtleties and nuances of relationship management, including the duty of good faith.

What is the duty of good faith and how can it best be described? Good faith requires that neither party evade the "spirit" of the transaction so as to deny a party the expected benefit or "fruits" of the transaction. Good faith is based on honesty in fact. However, good faith does not protect a party from having exercised bad judgment or having gambled and lost. Nor is it ever "bad faith" to insist upon the strict application of the contract or to take advantage of a good deal. It is perfectly reasonable to insist on and hold the other party to the precise terms of the agreement.

Examples of bad faith include:

(i) intentional misrepresentation,
(ii) dishonest or misleading behavior,
(iii) exercising a right or advantage you are not entitled to and did not bargain for,
(iv) failing to give reasonable notice of a breach or intention to terminate so as to allow the other party to remedy the breach or mitigate damages.

A threshold question addresses when the duty of good faith applies. Most courts impose the duty of good faith after a contract is signed. Caveat Emptor (buyer beware) still applies to the law of the land when it comes to negotiation between merchants. Of course, this is not to say that negotiators can or should engage in fraud or fraudulently induce others to sign contracts with dishonest intent. But fraud implies a more specific and concrete level of dishonesty than the mere lack of good faith.

A note of caution – because this duty of good faith is vague, even courts may have varied interpretations. In addition, decisions tend to be fact sensitive and case specific. Know the facts and how your local courts view the issue. Particularly in the case of discretionary rights or duties (e.g., the unilateral right to cancel orders or terminate for convenience), special care needs to be paid to the obligation to act in good faith. Bear in mind that "merchants" (those in the business of buying and selling goods) are often judged by both the subjective (a reasonable belief) and an objective (actual reasonable behavior under the circumstances) standard when it comes to good faith.

Finally, courts may scrutinize behavior in the context of good faith where one party contains a monopoly on information or the transaction involves a "fiduciary" duty, as in the case of certain agreements such as franchise, joint ventures, employment or distribution agreements.

Closely related to the notion of good faith is the transgression of commercial fraud. Commercial fraud goes far beyond the trip wire of good faith. It involves a representation of material fact that is false and relied upon with resulting damages. It also involves bad intent on the part of the person making the representation. Mere "puffery", however, is not fraud. Puffery is frequently used to describe the exaggerations reasonably expected from a seller regarding a degree of quality or performance that typical consumers would not take seriously, e.g. "the finest in the world".

Carlill vs. Carbolic, EWCA. CIV. 1 (1892) is another old English contract law decision which dealt with representations regarding the effectiveness of a flu remedy. The court held that the maker's comments went beyond mere puffery and amounted to a binding legal commitment because of the level of detail and specificity. However, in some jurisdictions making statements with reckless or willful disregard as to their truth (or "grossly negligent" statements) can qualify as fraud. Again the line is not always clear.

While fraud typically involves an intentional false material representation relied upon by another party to his or her detriment, fraudulent concealment can arise where no false statements have actually been made, but actions have been taken to hide information or a problem such as a defect or other disadvantage. Fraudulent concealment involves the failure to disclose a material fact intended to induce an incorrect belief or conclusion. It is that active concealment that constitutes the fraud.

Good faith, fraud and fraudulent concealment are, as noted, very fact sensitive and case specific determinations which defy elimination by process alone. This requires continuous training and monitoring. Your staff needs to be continuously reminded about and instructed by the leadership and counsel on how to "stay on the side of the angels".

GETTING STARTED: PREREQUISITES

"A good beginning makes for a good ending", as the saying goes. Before you let anyone be involved in your supply or demand chain process make sure they understand and are prepared to follow basic foundational prerequisites as set by your organization. Some of these potential prerequisites are discussed below.

<u>Standards of Integrity</u>. A keen understanding of and appreciation for the organization's standards of integrity is critical. These days, most employees will move, over the span of their careers, to several different employers. Different employers may have different standards of integrity. For example, some employers permit supply / demand chain professionals to accept modest or token gifts from suppliers. Others forbid it. It is essential that your "new employee" ("C level", i.e., executive and below) understands and follows your organization's standards of integrity to the letter.

<u>Delegation of Authority</u>. The same considerations apply to the organization's particular procurement procedures including, for example, the appropriate delegation of authority ("DOA") protocol. It is vitally important for all employees to understand not only the limits of their authority but who actually has the authority to contractually bind your organization. Watch out for and guard against the "Apparent Authority" trap. If you allow individuals to act as if they have authority and third parties reasonably rely on your actions or inactions in this regard, courts may deem that you have created apparent authority in individuals who do not have actual authority. See discussion below.

Apparent Authority. It seems like common sense that everyone automatically knows the limits of their authority and who has the power to make what decisions. However, this is not always the case and many organizations every year find themselves in the "Apparent Authority" trap whereby an employee (knowingly or unknowingly) has made a contractual commitment he or she was not authorized to make. The result is a binding commitment because the counterparty reasonably relied on the acts or omissions of your organization. This is a problem not only with new employees but often with longstanding employees as well who may have fallen into a pattern of behavior which has evolved over the years and your organization has never questioned or challenged.

Transaction Review. Likewise, each and every employee should understand the organization's Transaction Review Process ("TRP") to ensure that all "bases are covered" and all "boxes checked" by the right subject matter experts. Again, this seems simple in theory but is actually difficult in practice. For example, when does the organization require legal, accounting, insurance or risk management review or input? This question has both temporal and qualitative considerations from the standpoint of timing or thresholds. How much time is needed for review or input by subject matter experts? The dollar threshold amounts are questions that need to be answered by each individual organization depending on their needs, capabilities and tolerance for risk. Likewise, organizations should have a means to identify potentially "high risk" transactions and handle them appropriately given the level of risk tolerance of the organization.

Privity of Contract. In addition, all individuals involved in your process need to understand the principle of privity of contract. Simply stated, you only have a deal with the named entity on the contract and, absent a parental guarantee, parents or affiliates are not bound. Don't fall into the trap of not understanding that the liability of organizations is limited to their assets. Understand who you are doing business with and what their financial resources and capabilities are.

Change / Self-Management. Change is inevitable. Your employees need to understand and follow the approved change order process set forth in your contract documents. Informal changes and "hand-shake" deals always come back to haunt an organization. Closely related is the overuse of letters of intent and other preliminary agreements that put off the hard work of reaching an agreement before accepting the delivery of any goods or services. Remember, "agreements to agree" are unenforceable. Don't let yourself fall into the trap of using "to be agreed upon" language or an "it's understood" mentality in your contracts.

Conduct / Communications. Conduct can affect contract rights. Your employees need to understand and follow the contract if you expect courts to enforce it. Casual interpretations based upon superficial or incomplete knowledge of the facts and then memorialized in loosely worded emails can undermine the enforceability and effectiveness of well-crafted contract documents. Moreover, emails are not the place to express humor, anger or innuendo, resolve disputes or waive contract rights. Always assume that one day your worst enemy may read and use your emails against you.

It bears repeating that good contract management begins with self-management. That means that employees need to understand the consequences of their conduct. Especially in the case of employees working as buyers or procurement professionals, the risk of apparent authority is much higher than for their counterpart "sales" representatives. As noted above, one area where this is especially apparent and can be exceedingly problematic is in casual ill-thought out email communications. Every employee needs to be instructed and periodically reminded that emails are discoverable, not always treated as confidential, easily misinterpreted and permanent in the sense that despite being deleted, they can be recovered electronically.

Contracting Protocol and Audits. Closely related to an organization's needs, capabilities and risk tolerance is the use of approved templates and the scope of discretion in tailoring these approved commercial terms and conditions. There also needs to be a process to measure and monitor whether the organization's sourcing tools and change management protocols are being followed. Frequent contract audits are a necessity.

Integration Clauses. Each and every employee (including executives) needs to know and understand that once a contract is signed only what is contained within the "four-corners" of the contract can be legally relied upon. Presentations, charts, emails, marketing materials, conversations, representations or the like are not part of the deal unless specifically incorporated by reference. Read and understand the "Entire Agreement" language at the end of every contract.

Good Faith. As previously noted, good faith needs to be part of every agreement and in fact the law implies and imparts that duty into each contract. It means honesty in behavior and allowing each party an opportunity to achieve the "fruits" of the transaction. However, following the letter of the contract is never bad faith.

Contract Terminology. "The beginning of wisdom is to call things by their right names", as the Chinese proverb goes. Contracts have their own language and terminology. Your employees need to know the difference between an "option", "offer", "firm offer" and "right of first refusal" as well as other terms commonly used in contracts. Moreover, words used in a commercial context may have a different meaning than when used in everyday context. For example, the word "delivery" can mean something very different in a commercial context than when used in everyday speech.

Employees should also understand that "penalties" should never be part of a contract since compensation is the remedy not punishment. In addition, terms such as "liquidated damages" are terms of art that have specific meaning and need to be used correctly and in the right context. Often overlooked is the importance of definitions in contract documents, either in the legal terms, in the scope or in other documents. For example, how a word like "Work" is defined not only affects the respective responsibilities of the parties in terms of what is to be performed or delivered, but also has implications under the indemnity and insurance provisions of the agreement. Likewise, how the parties choose to define "Force Majeure" has implications with regard to the termination and cancellation provisions of the agreement. Definitions need to be consistent since you don't want the lawyers defining something one way and the technical folks defining it another way. Also be on the lookout for "phantom" definitions that are not used in the agreement.

Proceeding to Playbook

Once management is satisfied that basic prerequisites have been met and are in fact being followed, the organization can move on to considering which steps in your supply / demand chain process need to be adopted, modified or eliminated.

The following *PLAYBOOK* steps are recommended as a starting point for evaluating / auditing your current procedures to determine whether they are in fact optimal. This will allow you to develop your own playbook and tailored tools best suited to your organization's needs. It is important to note that the specific steps an organization identifies in its Playbook are unique to that organization but can be based on the principles and techniques offered in this book. Likewise, the Desktops and Tools are only samples to be tailored to your organization's needs or, if more appropriate, re-drafted and re-written as necessary. Clearly laying out these steps, testing your assumptions and building templates is the essential process to promote consistency, collaboration and predictability in execution. Moreover, doing so allows for the implementation of computer technologies to create the digital infrastructure that can become your online playbook.

It may be tempting to dismiss the ideas of *PLAYBOOK* as "not needed here", under the mindset that "We are already plenty self-reflective and self-critical. Besides, we already have an effective computerized contract management system." Any such organization is truly blessed. A few questions may quickly lead to a different conclusion. For example, are you satisfied with the number of change orders arising out of your contracts? Excessive change orders can be an indicator of poor contracting including poor scope of work definition. Is your organization clear on when to use a purchase order versus a more formal contract? Does your organization often permit contractors to start work or suppliers to deliver goods before contracts are signed? The answers to such questions may be indicators that process improvement (*PLAYBOOK*) should be considered.

PLAYBOOK STEPS

The following steps are offered for illustrative purposes. Your organization may choose to add, delete or change the order of these steps. In addition, there may be pre-steps to Step 1 such as obtaining market intelligence, assessing staff capabilities or the like.

STEP 1:   Obtain Client Requisition

Businesses that are exceptionally well-organized can, to some degree, anticipate a client's procurement needs but as a practical matter most transactions begin with a client requisition. It is incumbent upon the supply chain organization to understand the client's needs and ensure that the requisition as provided meets those needs. This may be an iterative process that requires knowledge of the business, an understanding of the individuals involved and the market for the goods or services being sought. All are necessary, including asking the right questions and understanding the schedule.

Always ask, and confirm, whether the client in fact has authorization to spend money. Many times a client will make requests in connection with seeking budget authorization. Determine whether the client has authorization to spend money or is simply seeking information or your support to obtain authorization. It's important to understand and appreciate the distinction from a process standpoint.

STEP 2: Determine Whether to Bid

A threshold issue to be addressed is whether or not to competitively bid the transaction. If the decision is not to bid the transaction then a bid waiver should be obtained or prepared as appropriate, documenting the reasons for the decision. Of course not every transaction needs to be bid provided that an organization applies guidelines in terms of when to seek competitive bidding. These guidelines will vary with the organization's needs.

Remember that competitive bidding is not always about getting better (cheaper?) pricing or higher quality. Sometimes it's about getting more favorable risk allocation. For example, if your organization is heavily dependent on engineering services, would you rather get rates at $5 an hour less or have a better remedy for defective work? Having your engineering services supplier be responsible for "corrective construction" (i.e. not just for the cost of re-performing the services but also for the cost incurred as a result of the defective services) might be much more valuable than a lower rate.

STEP 3: Develop the Scope of Work / Supply ("SOW / SOS")

Critical to the success of any transaction is the scope of work / supply that governs what will be performed or provided and what result is to be expected. It is tempting for supply and demand chain management professionals to "wash their hands" of the requirement for a solid scope of work / supply under the rationale that "this is a matter for the technical folks". Not true.

Yes, good scope writing requires technical expertise. However, the irony is that technical experts are not necessarily good scope writers since they are often the victims of too much knowledge. This yields to assumptions about what the reader should know and understand about the scope of work. In addition, scope writing takes time and writers easily fall prey to the seduction that "It's understood". Don't let your people avoid the hard work of hammering out a good scope. Additionally, don't fall into the trap of allowing a bidder to write the scope of work. Ideally, proposals are the starting point, not the end point, for developing sound work scopes. Great care needs to be taken in how you write your scope or request for proposal. For example, if you specify that something needs to be built only in a certain way or "as close as possible" to some location, you may needlessly narrow possibilities, drive costs and create ambiguity. Even where an organization does not have the technical sophistication to write a technical scope, the scope can be written in terms of the "result" to be achieved. Here is where desktop tools become critical to an organization's success. A desktop tool on how to write and structure a scope of work not only promotes consistency, but provides a framework for success.

It is important to develop an SOW / SOS early in the process since it will dictate much of what follows. Negotiating contract terms and conditions without a good SOW / SOS makes it impossible for either side to understand the costs and risks that need to be addressed as a prerequisite to coming to any commercial agreement. Although it is best practice for the purchaser to develop the SOW / SOS there may be occasions when a contractor or original equipment manufacturer ("OEM") ends up, in effect, writing the document. In such cases you must take ownership of the document and ensure it is scrubbed of any commercial content or other provisions which are inconsistent with your organization's best interests. "Make it your own", as the saying goes.

[See Attachment to Step 3: Developing SOWs / SOSs]

STEP 4: Perform Stakeholder Mapping / Scheduling

Stakeholder mapping is important because it allows the organization to define its needs, requirements and schedule.

This is the time to focus on the schedule for the project's work or delivery of the goods. Logically, it makes sense to have an understanding of the SOW / SOS before undertaking to create a schedule. The SOW / SOS, as well as the determined schedule will affect the cost / budget. Early on and certainly with the delivery of the proposal, there should be a "Level 1" Schedule. This is sometimes called a "milestone level" schedule and consists of targets that are scheduled to be met by specific dates so that progress can be measured. It provides the end-to-end framework on which to develop a more refined and detailed schedule. A "Level 2" schedule adds a further layer of detail and is sometimes used. However, within [X] days of contract signing, an early deliverable should include a "Level 3" schedule acceptable to the company with a high degree of detail outlining the monitoring, management and measuring of activities to meet project or transaction deadlines. Your scheduling experts can define for you the appropriate format and level of detail for job specific schedules and provide you with descriptions distinguishing one from another.

STEP 5:   Obtain Fiscal Authorizations

Before the process gets too far along, it is important to confirm and ensure that the expenditures for the purchase being contemplated have in fact been authorized. Bear in mind that there is also a cost to administering and managing the transaction post execution. The "cost" of the contract, therefore, is not simply the price set forth in the agreement, but in fact includes the cost of managing the transaction from "cradle-to-grave" throughout its life cycle.

STEP 6:   Define Commercial Strategy and "Legal Landscape"

Early in the process, a well-defined commercial strategy needs to be followed. Every transaction will have its own unique aspects, but a consistent method of evaluating the best commercial strategy should be followed.

This starts with deciding whether to use a simple purchase order or a detailed contract.

Defining and setting commercial strategy requires, among other things, an assessment of the legal landscape for the transaction. For example, for transactions under US law, consider whether this will involve goods falling under the provisions of the Uniform Commercial Code ("UCC"). Remember that some transactions are "mixed" involving a combination of goods and services and whether the UCC applies may not be entirely clear with courts applying the so-called "predominant nature" test. Likewise, if the transaction involves international trade or foreign-based counter parties, special considerations may apply.

Of course, significant or high risk transactions should never be done via purchase order (which essentially contemplates an exchange of forms, and in the event of a conflict between each party's commercial terms and conditions, the applicable provisions of the Uniform Commercial Code applied). This is no way to contract for significant procurements of either goods or services. Limit the use of purchase orders as the primary contract document to routine low risk purchases for mass produced items.

Now is also the time to consider risks and risk mitigation steps. For example, does the transaction expose the organization to "concentration risk" leaving it too dependent on a single product, service or supplier? Note that due-diligence on risk is an ongoing process that will need to be followed with appropriate steps during the entire transaction life cycle.

Entering into contracts involves identifying and evaluating the risks, as well as strategizing to eliminate or minimize those risks. Asking the following questions can help in that process:

1. What are the risks? Identify and make a list of the risks.

2. How likely is it that the risk will occur? Evaluate the risks in terms of probability.

3. What are the consequences of taking (or avoiding) the risks? Evaluate the risks in terms of their consequences.

4. Does the potential reward justify the risks? Weigh the potential for success against the consequences of failure.

5. What can be done contractually or otherwise to eliminate or minimize the risks? Make a list of ways to manage or control the risks.

6. Is this a "high-risk, low-gain" transaction with a lot of risk for little gain? Avoid risking a lot to gain a little.

7. Does the probability of success justify the risks that are being incurred? Avoid risking more than you can afford to lose.

8. Is the party at risk able to both control and bear the risk? Identify who is at risk and which party or entity should bear the risk.

9. Is the risk "short-term" or does taking the risk have potential long-term consequences? Determine the duration of the risk.

10. Can the transaction be structured and administered to maximize "high-reward, low-risk" potential? Manage and control the risk.

Risk management also involves "self-management" in the sense that the whole team needs to be on the same page regarding both process and behaviors. Keep everyone focused on what is important and what could derail the effort, even if it means repeating the same message over time. Remember: "Repetition is the mother of all learning", as the saying goes. It does not "spoil the prayer".

[See Attachment to Step 6: Commercial Strategy / Legal Landscape]

STEP 7:   Identify Prospective Bidders

Early in the process, a well-defined bid list needs to be prepared. This list should be created based upon past experience and input from various stakeholders. It is important to articulate for your internal client base why certain bidders should or should not be considered. The bid list should be circulated for appropriate approval and documented accordingly. Avoid a messy "email trail" as the documentation for the bid list.

Now is the time to perform due-diligence on the supplier or contractor. Note that for long-term contracts due-diligence may need to be updated annually. Due-diligence may include risk assessment and classification of the services or products offered by the provider as "critical", "significant" or "non-essential". Due-diligence should include consultation with the departments involved as well as with the subject matter experts.

Use of business credit reporting agencies may also be helpful to obtain information concerning credit ranking and summaries, corporate registration and contact information, payment trends and predicted payment behavior, UCC and bankruptcy filings, liens or judgments against the business. These reports often contain valuable details about a business and pertinent facts regarding key personnel.

[See Attachment to Step 7: Approved Bidders List Template]

STEP 8:   Assess Confidentiality

It may be appropriate to obtain a confidentiality agreement prior to allowing a bidder to submit a proposal. Confidentiality agreements come in different formats and have slightly different objectives depending on the transaction. Some confidentiality agreements are reciprocal in nature and others protect only one party to the transaction. Depending upon the transaction, a high degree of confidentiality and care may be required. Although everyone believes they understand what information needs to be protected, the reality is that confidentiality agreements are often treated in a very cursory and casual way. This is a mistake and understanding confidential information and how to protect it, together with the use of the proper confidentiality agreement, is critical.

[See Attachment to Step 8: Confidential Information]

STEP 9:   Finalize Bidders

Once the proposed list of bidders has been circulated and a final list is developed and approved by the client, ensure that the appropriate protocol and delegation of authority is followed. This is a prerequisite to issuing requests for proposals ("RFPs").

STEP 10:   Begin Cycle-time Tracking

Many organizations utilize cycle-time tracking from RFP issuance to contract execution. This is the point at which you should start tracking time. Cycle time tracking is important since it allows the team to focus on the time it takes to complete the process thus maintaining leverage and momentum for quick closure. Progress can be tracked in MS Excel including RFP issue date, execution date, milestones or other key dates, contract termination and final closure, etc. It also allows for calendaring of events critical to the management of the transaction such as renewal or expiration dates for insurance and letters of credit.

STEP 11: Register Approved Bidders in Accounting / Finance System

Many organizations utilize one or more proprietary products such as SAP for tracking and managing suppliers. Now is the time to register bidders not previously in the system following the instructions as appropriate.

STEP 12: Determine Tax Liability

Often overlooked is the issue of sales or other tax liability and who pays it. Bids may quote a price and sometimes the quote includes sales or other tax liability and sometimes it does not. It is important to understand whether the quoted price includes sales tax or other tax liability to avoid confusion and permit a proper bid evaluation.

STEP 13: Consider Pricing

"Price" is not just what is paid at the time of initial purchase. One of the more difficult issues to deal with is managing price changes over time. Parties often use price adjustment clauses. However, these price adjustment clauses can often result in unintended consequences when changes in pricing are triggered by factors that do not affect a provider's cost. Consider alternatives to the so-called "consumer price index" or other such indices and ensure that an appropriate index is used or alternatives are explored.

[See Attachment to Step 13: Price Adjustments]

STEP 14: Select Commercial Terms

The RFP should contain the appropriate commercial terms and conditions being sought by the purchaser. Commercial terms and conditions are, in effect, price terms since the level of risk, quality specified, required insurance and the like all can have an impact on price. The right terms and conditions should be selected to ensure that your organization is appropriately protected given the nature of the transaction. Generally speaking, the entity best able to control or manage the risk should be the one assuming that risk. The contract's terms and conditions should reflect that approach.

STEP 15:   Manage Financial Risk

Closely related to the selection of commercial terms and conditions is the type of financial risk management warranted by the transaction. This could include retainage, progress payments tied to performance, letters of credit, parent guarantees and the like.

[See Attachment to Step 15: Financial Risk Management]

STEP 16:   Prepare and Issue RFPs / ITBs

Although you can start from templates for requests for proposals (RFPs) and the accompanying instructions to bidders ("ITB"s) it is best to tailor them to the appropriate transaction. It is important to ensure quality and consistency and not allow individual employees to go on a "frolic and detour" and create their own RFPs and ITBs. Good RFPs clearly identify how bidders should structure their bids and how the bids will be evaluated.

Of course, blindly following a template also has its risks. RFPs and ITBs from prior projects should not be used without proper vetting and tailoring. Remember that by issuing an RFP you are soliciting an "offer" subject to your acceptance. Make sure you request a "firm" offer, i.e., an offer that can't be withdrawn and stays open subject to your acceptance for a specified period of time (e.g., 90 days).

Although obvious, everyone should be reminded of how the RFP process fits into satisfying the elements of a contract. A contract is created when an "offer" is followed by an "acceptance" supported by "valuable consideration" for some "legal object or purpose" by "competent parties". Since offers empower the recipient, purchasers are in the business of collecting offers. An RFP is your request to the bidder to provide an offer to you. By "valuable consideration" we mean anything of value including a promise to do something (or in some cases even a promise to refrain from doing something, such as in the case of a release). Bear in mind that "competent parties" means legally competent, not necessarily technically or otherwise competent in the usual sense of the word. The point is that the RFP is not what ends up in the contract. It's simply the vehicle for requesting an offer. Also bear in mind that the information obtained via the RFP process is not automatically incorporated into the contract unless steps are taken to make it so. If a scope of work is not part of the RFP, the receipt of the offer can be used, through the negotiating process, to create the scope of work needed.

Early in the process, it is important to specify risk of loss and shipping terms. A key question in any transaction involves who will be liable in the event goods are damaged, destroyed or lost in transit. There are two typical scenarios: (a) only the parties to the transaction (buyer and seller) are involved and, (b) a common carrier (trucking, airline or shipping firm) is also involved. If only the buyer and seller are involved, risk of loss typically follows possession. In cases involving a common carrier, the answer of who bears the risk that goods are destroyed, damaged or lost in transit depends on the Free on Board ("FOB") point.

If goods are shipped FOB "origin", the purchaser is assuming the risk of loss once the goods are delivered to the common carrier. The purchaser could try to hold the carrier accountable, however this is difficult to do since their liability is typically limited by tariff. Geography may also make it problematic to pursue the common carrier. Moreover, carriers may or may not have financial or other assets.

Where the parties agree that delivery will be FOB "destination", it means that the seller bears the risk of loss until the goods are delivered to the specific destination. Where goods are shipped FOB destination, it is important to be as specific and detailed as possible. You may specify a room number or even geographic coordinate. FOB "NYC" or even "XYZ Corp." is far too vague. Note that ownership is not the determining factor when it comes to risk of loss in transit.

In addition, whether the UCC or INCOTERMS are used to describe shipping, it is important to understand what abbreviations mean. This can be complex. The key is to focus in on three basic things: (a) who bears the cost of shipment, (b) who owns the goods at a given point and (c) who is responsible for paying in the event the goods are damaged, destroyed or lost. There is no legal requirement to use the UCC or INCOTERMS abbreviations and parties are free to allocate the risk of loss in transit as they see fit using their own words. Finally, note that the risk of loss passes to the buyer only if conforming goods have in fact been shipped.

[See Attachment to Step 16: Sample RFPs / ITBs]

STEP 17: Manage the RFP Process

It will take time and effort (and a budget) to manage the RFP process. Essentially, purchasers collect offers in an effort to make the best choice possible. If the RFP has been done right, the process will yield conforming bids without (or with few) "exceptions", "clarifications" or "assumptions" which detract from the bid and create difficulties in evaluation. Questions need to be addressed on both a technical and commercial level but a single point of contact (or one for commercial questions and another for technical questions) should be designated to avoid bidders "shopping for answers". The purchaser's employees need to be knowledgeable about the risks of being contacted during a bid process and need to understand who should respond to avoid problems, maintain consistency and preserve the integrity of the bidding process. This requires instruction and training as well as supervision.

STEP 18:   Conduct Pre-Bid Meeting

It is important to conduct a pre-bid meeting and allow for a site inspection by the bidders if work is to be performed at a particular location. A template or checklist can be used to facilitate this process. Members of both the technical and commercial teams should be present to answer questions about the RFP.

STEP 19:   Receive Proposals

The next step is to receive proposals or responses from bidders declining to bid. These should be recorded in accordance with your organization's protocol.

STEP 20:   Confirm Bids are Complete and Note any Deficiencies

Notwithstanding excellent RFPs, it should be expected that certain bids will have deficiencies or exceptions that need to be highlighted and addressed. This is also where you address whether a "Round 2" is appropriate. A key consideration is how to handle "mistakes" in a bid. Generally, a bidder should not be allowed to change a bid after submittal even if the mistake was genuine. However, a bidder may be permitted to withdraw a bid without prejudice if it can be demonstrated that the mistake was unintentional or justifiable and did not result in any real harm to the recipient.

In a timely fashion, review all bids to confirm that they conform to the bid requirements, and provide quick feedback to bidders. Create the internal discipline to always give prompt feedback, especially regarding any deficiencies. If you wait too long to do so, the whole effort will lose momentum. Moreover, if you delay providing feedback on bid deficiencies you may give the impression that the matter is not important or even that the bidder is the only or preferred bidder, thereby losing leverage.

STEP 21:   Distribute Bids to Internal Stakeholders

Bids should be distributed to internal stakeholders. However, depending on the circumstances, not everyone needs to receive priced bids. The distribution of pricing information should be managed to ensure the integrity of the process.

STEP 22:   Prepare Bid Tab

A comparative analysis of the bids should be provided with recommendations to management and stockholders. Here again, consistency is important and an organization should have a form and format used across the organization. The evaluation factors should be agreed upon by the evaluation team before bids have been received and incorporated into the bid tab format.

[See Attachment to Step 22: Bid Tab]

STEP 23:   Perform Final Tax Review

Understanding the tax implications is critical before making any final decision. This is the time to again review which entity has what tax obligations and consult tax subject matter experts.

STEP 24:   Perform / Finalize Negotiation

Now is the time to perform or finalize negotiation on scope, price or terms, having previously developed your strategy for doing so. Again, proposals may contain information which should not be included in the final contract. For example, a proposal may include the seller's commercial terms and conditions contradicting those in the purchaser's contract. It would make no sense and in fact be very awkward to accept the proposal with that kind of information embedded within it.

From a process standpoint, it is very common for negotiating parties to exchange redlined versions of the contract documents with each party inserting its proposed changes, revisions, and re-revisions showing additional strikeouts ("red-lined"). Very quickly, the document becomes overly complicated and unworkable. Moreover, it is very easy to lose track of what version is being worked on.

The solution is simple: version control. One party, typically the purchaser, keeps a "master" version. It is that version that the purchaser sends back to the seller with accepted changes being proposed. In other words, the parties never "ping pong" the documents back and forth. Proposed changes are reviewed by the purchaser and either rejected or inserted into the master draft and sent back to the seller. The other reason to do this is that sometimes changes are made but not identified in the "redlined" version. Intentional or not, this is a real practical risk. The drawback to this process is that one party is going to have to read the entire document each time it is sent back to them. They would have to do this anyway because you cannot trust that all changes will be made or identified. This process saves both the purchaser and the seller having to reread all the documents each time they are sent back and forth. One party or the other is going to have to be inconvenienced.

During negotiations, it is often difficult to determine precisely when negotiations end and an agreement is reached. To avoid this problem, parties often specify that there is "no deal, unless and until a formal contract is executed by the parties' duly authorized representatives". This avoids misunderstandings. Almost anything is easier to get into than out of so control the moment of agreement very carefully.

It bears mentioning that only what ends up "within the four corners of the contract" is part of the deal. As specified in the contract's integration clause, only what is included in the contract, either directly or by incorporation, can be relied on as part of the bargain.

No commercial term or condition is more important than the scope and duration of the warranties applicable to the goods or services being purchased. Accordingly, use of a warranty checklist is recommended in the negotiating process to ensure that all important potential warranties are discussed.

[See Attachment to Step 24: Warranty Checklist]

STEP 25:   Evaluate Proposals
Each transaction will have unique requirements which demand specific evaluation. However, every transaction should be governed by certain general principles including certainty, specificity, and risk sharing / allocation. Bearing that in mind, every organization should develop its own overriding principles with regard to how proposals are to be evaluated and should apply those principles consistently.

[See Attachment to Step 25: Proposal Evaluation Principles]

STEP 26:   Prepare Letter of Recommendation
A letter of recommendation should be prepared by the client with the help and support of the supply chain team and technical experts as necessary. This letter of recommendation ("LOR") documents the transaction and permits a vehicle and record for executive sign-off. It is important to obtain such a memorialization since memories fade, executives come and go and individuals may not recall why certain decisions were made.

[See Attachment to Step 26: Letter of Recommendation]

STEP 27: Obtain Final Authorization / Sign-Off

As a prerequisite to the letter of recommendation ("LOR"), the appropriate individuals from legal, risk management, tax, insurance, and accounting / finance need to sign-off, as appropriate, consistent with the organization's protocol and delegation of authority ("DOA").

STEP 28: Develop Contact List

Each contract should include an emergency list containing the contact information for key players who may need to be reached at off or odd hours. This might include cell phone numbers and personal email addresses to ensure that communication can be made if circumstances warrant it.

STEP 29: Assemble Contract Documents

The completed contract documents should be assembled in their final form ready for approval, signature and filing.

STEP 30: Obtain Signatures

This step seems simple but actually involves a fair bit of planning / scheduling. Many executives delegate the negotiation and preparation of transaction documents to subordinates but require time to personally review the final documents prior to their execution. Different executives may have different time requirements but one thing is certain: if you ask an executive to sign a document with inadequate notice, it will not be well received. Know your internal clients and their needs. In addition, the counter party's schedule needs to be considered.

Many organizations require that each page of a contract be initialed by both parties. Often, the initialing of the more technical documents such as scope or schedule is left to each party's subject matter experts. Moreover, transaction documents for more complex contracts tend to be lengthy. It may take, from a practical standpoint, a fair bit of time to mechanically obtain all the necessary signatures and initials. Of course, this practical challenge becomes more significant if more than one original ("wet copy") is desired. Keeping and being able to retrieve a signed original is important. Often, multiple drafts are circulated and unless the signed original is available it may be difficult to determine whether the copy in hand is truly the final version. This is fundamental "version control" and also very important in the event of a dispute since signed originals are still preferred, if not required, by courts as the "best evidence".

For the executive signing the document, the dilemma faced is that in all likelihood the document has not been exhaustively read from cover to cover by that executive. Yet, he or she is expected to sign. When faced with this important responsibility, executives may require a "red-flags meeting" with appropriate staff to ensure that all due-diligence has taken place and all precautions will take place.

One final point. Consider carefully where the originals will be formally and permanently filed. Often, the corporate by-laws dictate this will be with the organizations corporate secretary. The point is to make sure the original signed copy (the so-called "wet copy") is available in the future.

[See Attachment to Step 30: Red-Flags Checklist]

STEP 31:   Issue Control Number

Most organizations use some sort of numeric system to identify the contract by number. Often a purchase order number is issued for administrative purposes only as a tracking mechanism or to facilitate payment. It is important to identify in the contract documents that the purchase order number is being issued for administrative purposes only and that any pre-printed terms and conditions on the P.O. are superseded by the contract language.

STEP 32: Update Cycle Time

Pause to update your organization's cycle time chart as appropriate and if applicable.

STEP 33: Capture Cost Reduction Information

This is the time to capture any cost reduction information as appropriate and if applicable.

STEP 34: Prepare Transaction Abstract

Once the transaction is complete, a transaction abstract should be prepared. This is often the first step in developing a contract management plan. The transaction abstract should contain the highlights of the key commercial and technical considerations or factors unique to the deal. This is also the place to note any particular risks that require special attention going forward. The transaction abstract provides not only a summary but also a reminder of key action dates to be calendared such as insurance certificates or letter of credit renewals or expirations.

[See Attachment to Step 34: Transaction Abstract]

STEP 35: Confirm Internal Distribution

Confirm who in fact will get a copy of the contract. Copies of fully executed contracts should be distributed to all those involved in managing the transaction as noted therein. This would include not only first line personnel and project managers, but also individuals involved in the overall management of the transaction such as invoice processing and payment. Although there is a cost associated with providing copies of such documents, the individuals involved in ensuring that the parties follow the terms and conditions of the agreement need to be informed and have copies readily available.

STEP 36: Distribute Signed Copies

Key employees who must live with the deal and are involved in managing the transaction post-execution, should each have a copy available. Although contracts may contain commercially sensitive information, generally, it is best to make copies readily available to support the everyday management of the transaction. It makes no sense to hold employees accountable for managing the transaction if they are not provided with copies of the contract. This would include the individuals responsible for reviewing invoices as well as claims for additional compensation. Pocket sized versions of the contract documents can be prepared for ease of reference.

STEP 37: Draft Rejection Letters

Following execution of the contract, the other bidders should be notified that an award has been made. It is always difficult deciding what and how much to say to the other bidders about why they were not successful. The key point here is to preserve the relationship and reinforce the belief that the competitive bidding process was fair. One of the factors to balance is providing an appropriate level of feedback while not undertaking an unduly burdensome responsibility or violating any confidences. Stay with the facts and be succinct. Use of standard language is helpful in communicating a consistent message.

[See Attachment to Step 37: Rejection Letter Template]

STEP 38: Create a Contract Management Plan

This step involves the development of a plan for managing the transaction after the deal is signed. The contract should not simply be "filed and forgotten" but instead managed through to completion, with rights and remedies appropriately exercised in a timely manner. Such a plan is known as a Contract Management Plan ("CMP"). Give thought to and begin the development of the CMP early in the process.

Just as there is no perfect contract there is no perfect CMP. What goes into the CMP is governed not only by the contract, but also by the systems and procedures the organization has in place. The level of the employee sophistication is also a factor in how detailed the CMP needs to be. That said, a CMP would typically include the following items:

1. An overview of the purpose of the contract with a clear identification of the parties.

2. Both parties' management teams with a clear identification of key personnel and a statement of their respective roles and responsibilities.

3. A well-defined protocol and checklist for kick-off before the start of work.

4. Communication protocols between the parties including both formal and informal communications as well as the process for technical direction.

5. Protocols for change management, consistent with the terms and conditions set forth in the contract, including how requests for changes or company-approved change orders are issued. This would address contract modifications which can only take place by following the agreed upon process as reflected in the contract documents and only when such change orders are formally executed by duly authorized company personnel. Change management is key to successful contract management. That includes keeping track of the status of requests for changes and the changes themselves. This sounds simple but is actually

difficult in practice. A proper change management system includes a process for identifying the date a change request is received, identification of its status as "under investigation", "responded to", "accepted", or "rejected". The number and scope of change requests as well as change orders should be analyzed in terms of their frequency and extent and may be an indication of poor planning, inadequate scope articulation, or poor contract management. This is an area for a "lessons learned" post-contract assessment. The best commercial terms and conditions and work scopes are meaningless if proper change management is not adhered to. Incorporating a "change request form" requirement with specific information and due dates as part of the process is crucial. If the change request is granted this results in a "change order".

6.   A process for monitoring, measuring and reporting contract performance using the metrics called for and established in the contract such as Key Performance Indicators ("KPI"s). KPIs are measurable values used to demonstrate how effectively a project or contract is making progress and achieving both its targets and objectives. What is measured and monitored will differ depending upon the nature of the transaction (or even the department measuring performance). Typically, KPIs are tied to progress (as opposed to being expressed in purely financial terms e.g., "dollars" or some other currency denomination). Everyone on the team needs to understand what is being measured and why; with responsibility and accountability assigned to the appropriate person(s). KPIs should be designed to encourage positive effects on performance and corrective action with

appropriate frequency of reporting. It goes without saying, that ill-conceived KPIs will take things in the wrong direction. Measuring or rewarding the wrong thing (or useless measuring), is often the hallmark of a dysfunctional organization. The key is to focus on controllable events. Since people will act based on what is being measured, good or bad, be on the lookout for the unintended consequences of poor KPIs.

7. A process for controlling (and documenting) the point at which goods or services are deemed "accepted." Acceptance is something that needs to be done carefully after appropriate inspection, determination or testing, confirming that the goods provided or services performed in fact conform to the contract requirements. Once goods or services are accepted, payment is owed unless it can be proved they did not conform to the contract. You must also give timely notice of breach in the event of non-conformance. The point, however, is that mere receipt of goods or services does not necessarily mean acceptance. There should always be a reasonable period of time available under the contract to determine whether acceptance is appropriate and a clear methodology for documenting acceptance. Without a clear protocol, acceptance can be deemed to have occurred by the passage of time or some other conduct. For example, if one of your employees signs a receipt at the loading dock indicating that your organization has accepted the goods, that could be a problem. In such situations, it may be best to instruct your employees to simply sign as "acknowledging receipt only." The point is that neither payment nor receipt necessarily means acceptance. The moment of acceptance

is something that needs to be carefully managed as part of your contract management protocols.

8. Identification of key vulnerabilities or areas of risk, with plans for dealing with contingencies. During the execution phase of a contract, consider periodic mini-audits. Although most contracts have audit rights, it can be difficult to obtain people's attention once the contract or project is over. In addition, no good can come from failing to catch either under or over charges and such monies can be difficult to recover once time has passed.

9. A process for ensuring that all company employees understand the concept of privity, namely that the company's contractual relationship is with the contractor and not the contractor's subcontractors or suppliers of any tier, thereby avoiding the risk that company employees would direct the subcontractors or suppliers, or make any promises or commitments to them.

10. A process for ensuring that all company employees understand the risks of apparent authority; namely, that individuals should only act to the extent and within the limits of their actual authority and never assume or act as if they (or others) have authority which they do not.

11. A well-defined closeout process to ensure that all deliverables are in fact compliant, completed, and received and that the contract has been fully honored.

12. An audit of the transaction and "lessons learned" exercise.

Essentially, the purpose of a CMP is to implement an effective coordinated team approach for managing the contract. As noted above, the CMP is an internal document. Each party would have its own CMP. This is because the company and contractor have fundamentally different rights and obligations under the contract, despite having some shared objectives. Each party keeps the other "in line" by upholding the contract. Accordingly, each party should have its own CMP administering the technical, commercial, financial and other aspects of the contract with the objective of managing and mitigating risk, making the appropriate changes following contract protocols, documenting issues and resolutions, managing cost, schedule and performance and addressing emergent issues as needed.

A CMP is especially important given contracting's "dirty little secret" - namely, that a contract can be affected by what one does or says as well as what is written. "How can this be?", you may ask, given the very strict language found in all good contracts that the written documents contain the parties' entire and only agreement, which cannot be changed except in writing via formal change order. The answer has to do with the notion of "estoppel". Estoppel can be either "promissory" or "equitable". Both involve a representation, reasonable reliance upon such representation and resulting damage or detriment.

Under promissory estoppel, statements made to another party can be enforced even when they contradict a prior written agreement where: (a) a clear and definite promise is made with the expectation that it be relied upon and (b) the promise is reasonably relied upon with resulting damage or detriment.

Under equitable estoppel, statements (or sometimes even silence), acts or omissions can be the basis of a claim where such representations or conduct are made to: (a) intentionally induce action or under circumstances in which that action would likely be induced and (b) a good faith reliance on such behavior to that person's detriment or damage.

As noted, good contract management begins with good self-management. Nowhere is this more aptly demonstrated than in the use of email. Email is a powerful tool but so easily and often overused and misused. It's power is partly due to how easy it is to use, mimicking the convenient informality of speech but with the consequence of creating a permanent written record which may have been based on incomplete information or casual thought. Yet, there it sits – "carved in the stone" of the internet and (despite any efforts to delete), always retrievable given enough time, treasure and effort. Moreover, displays of emotion or humor are usually inappropriate in business emails and can create mischief. Consider establishing an email protocol.

Note that "But I sent an email..." is never an acceptable excuse when something didn't get done, got missed or messed up. If something is really important, confirm in person not only the receipt of information but also that understanding has occurred and action has resulted. The simple act of transmitting a message will be meaningless if the recipient "didn't get it", either physically or mentally. Do not assume people understand, or even read, your emails.

Part of the challenge in contract management is managing both the commercial (contractual) as well as the professional (personal) relationship. It goes without saying that personal relationships are critical to success in the business world and goodwill is priceless. However, one cannot depend on positive relationships (or even friendships) as a basis or substitute for a formally negotiated contract. Parties to a contract need to treat each other with respect and have honest discussions about interpreting what the contract means in the face of unavoidable ambiguities, but never allow the relationship to erode contract rights. This only leads to losing your contract rights and damaging the relationship. Moreover, relationships and even individuals may change, but the contract stands firm in the face of such shifting sands. Don't fall into the trap of allowing contractual obligations to be ignored or blurred based on relationships. No good can or will come of it. Courtesy, respect and consistency is the path to trust and success in both contracts and personal relationships. The consistency comes from both parties honoring the contract they entered into.

[*See Attachment 38: "Change Management Process"*]

STEP 39:   Sponsor Kick-Off Meeting

Use of a checklist before performance starts is a useful tool to ensure all key beginning steps are taken in order to have a successful transaction. It is especially useful at this point to have a meeting with the individuals involved in sending as well as paying invoices. It is not unusual for there to be confusion with regard to initial invoices. Delaying payment or mistakes in payment benefits no one. Now is the time to review the rules and protocols as set forth in the contract for issuing and processing payments. This ensures prompt and accurate payment. Of course, the company's internal team should have had its internal kick-off meeting a long time ago.

In the event you're dealing with trade unions, an early determination needs to be made regarding what labor contract the crafts will be working under. The unions must decide this. The owner doesn't attend these meetings but needs to ensure that they actually occur so that all the trade unions are in alignment regarding how the work will be performed from a labor relations standpoint, i.e., under local labor agreement, project specific labor agreement, or existing national labor agreements such as the National Maintenance Agreement ("NMA").

[See Attachment to Step 39: Kick-Off Checklist Template]

STEP 40:   Monitor Performance Under the Contract

Post execution follow-up to monitor performance is a key success factor in any transaction. This has multiple facets. Progress in terms of performance of the work and adherence to milestones is important. However, ensuring that payments are made promptly, correspondence is responded to in a responsive and timely manner and that expenditures are monitored are likewise critical. All this is part of monitoring performance after the contract is signed to ensure that both parties are adhering to their respective responsibilities and exercising their rights and remedies in an appropriate manner. This is where the CMP comes into play.

Remember that "active management" of the contract will be required. There is an old saying in project management that "It takes at least three attempts" in order to get anything done, e.g., three communications… email, voice mail and in-person. Repeat as necessary.

STEP 41:   Address Claims and Manage Change

No matter how well-written the contract may be, changes and claims are inevitable. This may include warranty claims by the company or claims by the contractor alleging additional compensable expenditures or cost of delays. Reference to the contract, collection of the facts and prompt notice and responses are the keys to success. Of course, asking the right questions when faced with a claim is the first important step.

Disciplined coordination with subject matter experts is also essential in addressing claims. This must be done with proper coaching to ensure a consistent method of response based on the facts. Guard against premature opinions based on inaccurate or incomplete information. Moreover,

64

an accurate log must be kept for each claim and status as well as the disposition of same through the project lifecycle. Timely correspondence is critical.

Without a clear and definitive change management process incorporated into the contract, the realities of living with the deal may become challenging. A good deal can be lost or undone through poor contract management.

[See Attachment to Step 41: Claims Letter Templates]

STEP 42: Closeout the Contract

Contract closeout must not be overlooked. It is essential to have a process or checklist to follow to ensure that all the deliverables have been provided including all associated documents (operating, maintenance or training manuals and the like) submitted. Use of contract closeout checklist is helpful.

[See Attachment to Step 42: Contract Close-Out Checklist]

STEP 43: Release Liens

Throughout the process, periodic partial release of invoicing for liens should be provided by the contractor as condition of receiving progress payments. At the end of the project / contract, a final release of liens or any claims is required prior to final payment.

STEP 44: Return LOC / Retainage

At the end of the project (or applicable warranty period), whatever security has been posted by the contractor under the contract to ensure performance should be returned as outlined under the contract. Remember that the original letters of credit ("LOC"s) must be returned to the contractor or the contractor's bank as specified in the contract. This means that while the company is holding the LOC, it should be kept in a safe place. Likewise, if security has been provided in the form of retainage, it should be returned as provided under the contract.

STEP 45:   Make Final Payment

The final invoice should be paid once accompanied by the final release of liens as noted above. The final release of liens should be written broadly enough to include all potential claims against the company by the contractor. A "close-out" should be final.

STEP 46:   Assess Performance

Once the project or transaction is over, a performance assessment should be made.

STEP 47:   Review Lessons Learned

At the conclusion of every significant project or transaction a "lessons learned" document(s) should be issued so that improvements can be made and mistakes are not repeated. It should be noted that lessons learned must be based on facts and not simply pure opinion or unwarranted second guessing.

[See Attachment to Step 47: Lessons Learned]

STEP 48:   Determine Whether the Contract is "Material"

Contracts or agreements, whether entered into or renewed by firms regulated by the Securities and Exchange Commission ("SEC"), which are "Material" are subject to SEC disclosure requirements. This generally applies to contracts entered into after August 23, 2004. Check with counsel. Material contracts are other than those made "in the ordinary course of business". The SEC does not define the term "Material" nor suggest the relevant factors to be used for making materiality determinations. This requires management's judgment on a caseby-case basis. Contracts will not be considered to be "ordinary course" if they involve:

- material leases;
- an officer, director or major holder;
- acquisitions or sales exceeding 15% of consolidated assets; or
- contracts on which the registrant's business is substantially dependent.

Disclosure is required upon execution, even if the contract / agreement is subject to contingencies. Moreover, any material change in "existing" material agreements must be reported and contractual confidentiality provisions is not a valid excuse for failing to make the necessary disclosure. Likewise, disclosure is required in the event of the termination of a material agreement (other than by operation of its terms). There may be similar statutes / regulations in other parts of the world, i.e., outside the United States.

STEP 49: Save Final Documentation

Collect final documentation pertaining to the transaction / project and store in accordance with corporate document retention procedures and policies.

BUILDING YOUR PLAYBOOK

Once you have identified the steps and sequence best suited to your organization's needs, you can build your own playbook. Consider the following Attachments as the kind of tools and desktops your organization can incorporate and rely on in the custom playbook you create.

Note that each step in your playbook should be identified with an associated accountable person or persons. In addition, each step should have the appropriate resource in the form of a desktop, checklist or other tool readily available for reference via a file link. This ensures that everyone is "on the same page" and has ready access to the knowledge and information necessary for an optimal transaction with "cradle-to-grave" contract management every step of the way. Your playbook should be geared to the level of sophistication and capabilities of your employees. As that level of sophistication and capabilities changes, your playbook can be modified accordingly.

ATTACHMENT TO STEP 3 - DEVELOPING SOWS / SOSS

<u>Instructions for using this Desktop:</u>

Insert instructions specific to your organization's needs and requirements.

1. INTRODUCTION

The scope is the key aspect of any procurement whether for goods, services or both. The work to be performed by the contractor is typically referred to as the Scope of Work ("SOW") whereas the goods to be delivered by a supplier is typically referred to as the Scope of Supply ("SOS").

The Scope should have well-defined deliverables that can be objectively measured.

A simple process for preparing high quality and effective Scopes is outlined below:

1.   Introduction
2.   Getting Started

3.   Collecting Your Thoughts

4.   Mapping the Scope Process

5.   Organizing Your Scope

6.   Applying Best Practices to the Process

7.   Referencing/Incorporating Other Documents

8.   Drafting Your Scope of Work using a Template

9.   Applying the Checklist to the First Draft of the Scope

The process outlined above can be used for developing the scope as part of a Request for Proposal ("RFP") or in evaluating a bidder's proposal. Often the preparation of the scope is left to the individual discretion of the author. This leads to inconsistency and differing approaches. This Desktop provides a platform to promote consistency and avoid errors.

Having a well thought out process consistently applied throughout the organization will reduce risk, improve productivity and facilitate the preparation of high quality scopes.

2. GETTING STARTED

This Desktop is designed to be used to prepare scopes for large or small transactions regardless of the individual's prior level of experience in writing scopes. However, preparing scopes does require some knowledge of the subject matter of the purchase.

What is a Scope?
The Scope is that part of a contract that defines what the person or entity (e.g., contractor, supplier, or consultant) is to provide, perform or otherwise accomplish.

For ease of reference we will use the term "contractor" in this text. A scope states the **desired outcome** to be delivered by the contractor in terms of the required result. The focus is on what is to be accomplished as opposed to dictating how the work is to be done.

Why are Scopes so important?
Scopes are a key part of any transaction and form the **basis for pricing**. Scopes are also relied upon in competitive bidding and used to calculate estimates, set budgets and measure performance. A good scope also helps **avoid, minimize and manage claims, changes and delays**. Scopes are part of a legal document and may one day be read and interpreted by judges or jurors.

What should not be included in the Scope?
Do not include legal, financial, compensation or risk allocation issues in the scope. Those issues should be addressed in the contract commercial terms and conditions, e.g., consider the following extract from a Scope of Work:

73

"If a utility is breached during test dig or construction, Contractor shall immediately notify the Company. For any utility that is shown on the Drawings, the Contractor shall be responsible for the cost and repair of any damaged utility."

In the above example, the first sentence may be appropriate to include in the Scope of Work since it is providing direction to the contractor in the event of a utility breach. However, the second sentence is inappropriate since it could be interpreted to mean that the contractor will be compensated for utility breaches that were not depicted on the drawings. If that is the intent, those risk allocation and compensation issues are best addressed in the commercial terms and not in the scope.

Likewise, do not include RFP requirements or language in the scope. RFP documents, including Instructions to Bidders ("ITBs"), are solicitation documents and not part of the scope. This is because the scope deals with what the contractor is to accomplish after the contract is signed whereas the RFP and ITB deal with the process by which the parties will reach agreement. For this reason, do not use the term "Bidder" in the Scope of Work documents.

In addition, do not include definitions in the scope that are inconsistent with or duplicative of those found in the commercial terms and conditions, such as "Work", "Company", "Equipment" or "Contractor". However, definitions or abbreviations of technical terms or standards are appropriate as part of the scope.

When do you need a Scope?

Scopes are most appropriate when services, systems or specially manufactured goods are being purchased. Scopes may not be as critical where routine mass produced articles or materials are being bought. However, where an equipment purchase requires installation, training or both, consideration should be given to preparing a scope. In effect, the purchase of a complex piece of equipment requiring specialized installation or training, or the manufacture of unique specialized items can be thought of as a "project" with its associated complexities.

Why not have the Bidder prepare the Scope?

It is always best to put things in your own words and to go through the discipline of independently thinking through your needs. Contractor's proposals often contain "exceptions", "assumptions", "clarifications" or extraneous materials. They may become outdated or need to be revised. When working from a contractor's proposal, review it for outdated or incorrect information or content which is inconsistent with your objectives. A good scope makes the proposal obsolete and unnecessary. Good commercial practice dictates that proposals do not become contract documents and the scope is conformed to reflect those portions of the proposal desired by the company.

How is the integrity of the process protected?

Particularly when scopes are going to be used as part of a competitive bidding process, all bidders should have equal access to information and the same chance for success. Be on guard for offers on the part of prospective bidders to assist in the development of the scope. This could lead to an actual or apparent unfair advantage. If a particular contractor is hired specifically to develop the scope, that contractor should probably not be allowed to bid on that scope. This avoids the appearance of impropriety.

Does your Scope need a Table of Contents?

Yes. Every good scope has a Table of Contents and each paragraph is numbered. This is an essential part of organizing the presentation of information in an effective and efficient manner. It also helps in the administration and management of the contract down the road. Avoid using bullets or un-numbered forms of identifying paragraphs or sections of the scope.

What if there is no time to prepare a Scope?

There should always be time to do things the right way. It is far better and more cost effective to avoid errors or omissions upfront, rather than correct them after the fact. However, in those situations where there is no time to prepare a scope and you must work from the contractor's proposal, there are steps you can take to mitigate the risks. These include deleting objectionable or irrelevant portions of the proposal and authorizing only a limited amount of work tied to specific deliverables.

3. COLLECTING YOUR THOUGHTS

What needs to be considered in writing scopes will vary depending upon the nature of the work to be performed. The following list is an example of what should be considered in preparing scopes. This list is not necessarily all inclusive and not all items listed need be considered in every scope. Since leverage is strongest at the beginning of the process, it is best to avoid omitting critical components.

1. What are the RESULTS to be achieved?
2. What is the current PERFORMANCE?
3. What are the specific DELIVERABLES?
4. What are the respective RESPONSIBILITIES?
5. What are the start, end, delivery and milestone DATES?
6. How is PAYMENT tied to the Contractor's PERFORMANCE?
7. What are the SITE, ACCESS, or ENVIRONMENTAL conditions?
8. What are the PERMIT, LICENSE, or REGULATORY requirements?
9. Where will DELIVERY or PERFORMANCE be made?
10. What are the SCHEDULING and REPORTING requirements?
11. What are the TEST and ACCEPTANCE criteria for completion?
12. What are the periodic INFORMATION requirements for the Scope?
13. What are the TRAINING and DOCUMENTATION requirements?
14. Who are the KEY PERSONNEL?

15. What are the STORAGE or LAYDOWN AREA requirements?
16. What are the required ACCURACY levels?
17. How RUGGED does the equipment need to be?
18. What are the TRANSPORTATION requirements?
19. What are the SPARE PART requirements?
20. What are the RELIABILITY requirements?
21. What are the MAINTENANCE requirements?
22. Are there special INSTALLATION requirements?
23. What is the WORK PLAN for getting the Scope done?
24. What are the UTILITY requirements?
25. Where are the user or operating MANUALS?
26. What are the COMPATIBILITY requirements?
27. What are the SERVICE LEVEL requirements?
28. What are the SOFTWARE / SOURCE CODE requirements?
29. What are the INSTALLATION / START-UP support requirements?
30. *Add additional items as appropriate*

4. MAPPING YOUR PROCESS

Developing the scope is part of the company's procurement process but the client's responsibility. In addition to having a well-defined process where everyone understands their respective roles and responsibilities, it is also important to understand and comply with any applicable procedures.

The steps outlined below are provided as an illustration of one possible high level approach. Follow the approach that meets your particular organization's needs and requirements depending upon the nature of the Scope.

1.   Determine the date by which a completed scope is required. The date must consider project lead time as well as the time necessary to negotiate the transaction and obtain all the reviews and approvals.

2.   Assign a designated individual the responsibility to prepare the scope.

3.   Read and be familiar with all the contract documents including the commercial terms and conditions, instructions to bidders and compensation provisions as well as other parts, exhibits or attachments that will make up the contract. This will avoid the risk of duplicative or inconsistent statements in the scope.

4.   Develop and update the scope through revisions based upon input and information from internal and external sources. It may be useful to understand the current level

of service or performance before beginning to write the scope.

5. Preparing scopes is often a multi-discipline process. Ensure the internal stakeholders have the opportunity for input. This could include risk managers, insurance specialists, lawyers, labor relations experts and others who have a stake in the outcome.

6. Obtain sign off and internal approval for the final scope to be included as part of an RFP or final contract as appropriate.

5. ORGANIZING YOUR SCOPE

As mentioned previously, every good Scope has a Table of Contents. The Table of Contents set forth below is an illustration of one possible approach.

The particular Table of Contents you use will depend upon the nature of the scope and how you choose to organize the document. High quality scopes are well organized and a Table of Contents improves and promotes clarity.

1. Definitions
2. Project Description
3. Intent and Objectives
4. Deliverables and Services
5. Test and Acceptance Criteria

6. General Requirements
7. Detailed Requirements
8. Performance Requirements
9. QA/QC Control Requirements
10. Schedule and Progress Reporting
11. Applicable Codes and Standards
12. Applicable Permits and Licenses
13. Project Management and Controls

14. Safety and Security Requirements
15. Site Requirements and Restrictions
16. Replacement Parts and Consumables
17. Shipping, Packing and Labeling Requirements
18. Training Needs for Existing and New Personnel

19. Operating / Maintenance Manuals and Information
20. Applicable Documents and Attachments to the Scope
21. Applicable Abbreviations and Acronyms used in the Scope
22. *Continue if and as applicable*

6. APPLYING BEST PRACTICES

Every organization has its own best practices based upon past "lessons learned". Apply those best practices to the scope process to avoid repeating past mistakes. The following practices are recommended for consideration.

Specify required results. Scopes are results-oriented and focus on and define success by a specific "result" in terms of what the contractor is to achieve. Specify the required result using active terms such as, "design", "develop", "perform", "produce" or "deliver" as opposed to a promise for a "level of effort" to try hard.

Set the right standards. A scope can contain "specification" standards, "performance" standards or a mixture of both. For example, the scope could require that the contractor comply with certain published industry codes or requirements or follow certain processes or procedures. The scope could also require that the product / system / facility meet specific performance or acceptance criteria or tests. Avoid setting the wrong standard, or setting standards that are too low or too high.

Clarity and consistency. The essential purpose of a contract is to set forth the respective responsibilities of the parties with precision for a predictable outcome. Accordingly, scopes need to be clear and consistent so that subsequent readers who were not involved in their preparation will have the same understanding as the original author(s).

Avoid ambiguity. Use simple, well-understood terms and words consistently and avoid colloquialisms or "buzz words". Saying it once correctly avoids ambiguity and needless repetition. Avoid using inexact terms like "etc.", "and/or", "unrestricted", "adequate" or the like. Use "shall" to express what the contractor is obligated to do and, if applicable, "will" to indicate what the owner is to provide. Don't use "should" or "may" to express required actions. Don't use abbreviations or acronyms unless they are defined in the scope or contract.

Watch out for multiple authors. Often, different sections of the scope are written by different persons at different times. Everyone has their own writing style and sometimes these multiple authors don't read what the others have written. The net result is a scope that is far from seamless and which lacks clarity and consistency. Have one person be in charge of proofreading and integrating the entire Scope by giving it a "cold" read.

Test your assumptions. The biggest mistake is to assume that the current project or procurement on which you are working is going to be "just the same" as the last one. The temptation is not to test that assumption and to either copy or "cut and paste" from the last project's scope. Better to apply good "lessons learned" rather than simply copy what was done before. The key is to tailor the scope to the particular circumstances.

Be Brief. The words "the" and "that" are two of the most overused words in the English language and are not always necessary. Examples of other ways to shorten contract documents include using: "To" vs "In order to..."; "If" vs "In the event that..."; "For" vs "In the amount of..."; "Whether" vs "Whether or not..."; "Any" vs "Any and all..." Nor is it necessary to continually repeat the phrase "It is understood and agreed that..."

Be Consistent. As noted above, proper use of definitions can promote consistency. Often contract documents require the work meet with the company's "approval" or "satisfaction" followed by words like "in the Company's sole judgment and discretion". Be consistent and if you mean "in the Company's sole judgment and discretion" either define "approval" or "satisfaction" to include that requirement or repeat the phrase every time.

Be Clear. Contracts often include cross references to other documents or sections of the contract. Have a consistent protocol for how you refer to those other documents or sections. If your contract contains exhibits that relate to a specific paragraph in the contract (e.g., "Article 23, par 1"), you can identify and tie that exhibit to the specific paragraph, e.g., "Exhibit 23.1". Avoid identifying different documents the same way (e.g., "Exhibit 1", "Attachment 1", "Appendix 1"). There should only be one "Exhibit 1", "Attachment 1", "Appendix 1". One way to do this is to have the contract refer to "Exhibits" and the Scope of Work refer to "Appendices" when it comes to referencing attachments. Clarity and consistency are also important for definitions. Consider having all definitions, both legal and technical, referenced in one place in the contract.

Be Careful About What is Incorporated by Reference. Not every document referenced in the scope necessarily becomes part of the contract. Some documents such as reports or information obtained from third parties may be provided for "informational purposes only". Ensure that you don't inadvertently include those documents as part of the contract or unintentionally "warrant" the accuracy or completeness of such documents.

7. REFERENCING OR INCORPORATING OTHER DOCUMENTS

While incorporating documents by reference can be a useful technique in putting together a Scope, it can also be a trap if not done correctly. The following steps can help avoid unintended consequences and manage the expectations of the parties.

1.   Ensure the documents do not contradict one another.

2.   Ensure the documents being incorporated are complete.

3.   Ensure the documents are clearly identified by title and date.

4.   Ensure the documents have been read as an integrated whole.

5.   Ensure the documents do not duplicate or reword information.

6.   Ensure the documents are correctly referenced throughout the contract.

7.   Ensure the documents are listed in one place in their order of precedence.

8.   Ensure that the documents are readily accessible to those who will be relying on them to manage the contract.

9.   Avoid wholesale incorporation of contractor documents before deleting objectionable conditions, assumptions, limitations, exceptions, or inconsistencies.

10.   Avoid incorporating documents that have yet to be created, which are subject to some future "mutual agreement" between the parties, or which can be unilaterally changed by the other party or by third parties.

11.   Decide whether certain documents should not be incorporated by reference into the scope but merely provided for "informational purposes only" as aid to the contractor's efforts. For example, subsurface investigation reports or underground drawings which may be inaccurate or incomplete should be provided for "informational purposes only" because the company does not want to inadvertently "warrant" their accuracy.

12.   Make sure appropriate safeguards are in place in the contract if sensitive or confidential information is to be provided in the scope.

8. DRAFTING THE SCOPE

The following template can be used as a guide in drafting Scopes.

EXHIBIT [SPECIFY] TO CONTRACT/PO [SPECIFY]
CONTRACTOR'S SCOPE OF WORK FOR
[SPECIFY PROJECT]

1. <u>Definitions.</u> The definitions set forth in the Company's commercial terms and conditions applicable to this transaction namely [specify] shall apply to this Scope of Work. In addition, the following terms shall be defined as set forth below:

    [Pay special attention to definitions. How words like "Work", "Materials", "Warranty" and the like are defined is crucial to a good scope. Remember that the scope is a part of the contract and that there may be definitions in other parts of the contract, particularly in the commercial terms and conditions. Make sure you don't trip over these definitions and that the key words are defined the same way in all sections of the contract. Avoid referring to the same thing using different terms. Consider having all definitions, both technical and commercial, in one place.]

2. <u>Project Description.</u>

    [Specify a general project description. This is a detailed overview of the project which should be expressed in summary fashion. Keep it to a paragraph or two.]

3.   Intent.

[Specify the intent of the contract. See example below.]

It is the intent of the parties that the Contractor engineer, design, procure, project manage, construct, test, start-up and commission a highly reliable (facility) in accordance with this Contract. The Contractor shall perform all of the Work specified or implied by this Contract in order to accomplish the intent of the parties. The Contractor's performance under this Contract shall include everything requisite and necessary to complete the entire Work notwithstanding the fact that every item involved may not be specifically mentioned. Details and items not indicated herein shall be adequately and properly performed by the Contractor at no extra cost, if such details or items are necessary to complete the Work.

[Specify the parties' responsibilities but avoid open-ended or vague commitments of facilities, personnel or resources on the part of the company (e.g., "Company shall provide...(limited defined specific list) . . . and Contractor shall provide everything else needed to perform the Scope of Work".) Avoid unwise commitments.

Be careful and specific when promising to provide equipment, facilities, manpower or other resources to assist the contractor. Generally, it is safest to limit the company's obligation to paying for work conforming to the contract.

If you do make commitments, make sure they are specific and limited. It is better to provide a defined lay-down area in the form of a map than to promise "adequate" lay-down area. If the company does have responsibilities under the contract, specify that unless otherwise specifically stated, any task or activity necessary to perform the work is the contractor's responsibility. Make it clear that any action or activity not clearly identified as the company's responsibility is the contractor's.]

4.   Objectives.

[Specify the objectives to be achieved in terms of the results, not just resources (e.g., hours to be worked), that the contractor is expected to deliver (e.g., "Contractor shall solve, correct, accomplish,..."). *Get an internal / Client sign-off on the equipment list.]*

5.   Deliverables.

[Provide a clear and complete description and specific quantity of items (e.g., equipment, hardware, software, etc.) that could be used as a checklist upon delivery. (e.g., part descriptions and part numbers)]

6.   Services.

[State when any services (e.g., installation, training, maintenance) are to begin and end, as well as where they are to be performed. Make sure you have due and end dates. If possible, start with clearly-defined user requirements and phase delivery to allow for testing and acceptance before the contractor moves on to the next phase.]

7.   Test and Acceptance Criteria.

[Specify how the deliverables will be tested to determine whether they conform to the contract requirements in terms of performance or capabilities. Any periodic testing or quality control review process should likewise be specified.]

8.   QA/QC Requirements.

[Specify the applicable quality assurance and quality control requirements.]

9.   The Schedule.

[Specify when each and every delivery is to take place and identify the components to be delivered and the services to be provided for that phase. For more complex projects, a level 1 baseline project schedule should be part of the contract with a level 3 schedule to be delivered within a prescribed period. Sometimes the schedule is a separate document or an attachment to the scope.]

10.   The Progress Reports.

[Specify any periodic milestone or progress reports that the supplier should provide to assist in measuring and monitoring performance. Specify the contents and format of the reports. Sometimes progress reporting is a separate document or part of project controls.]

11.   Project Management and Controls.

[Specify any project management and controls requirements. As noted above, sometimes this is a separate document or is located elsewhere in the contract.]

12.   Site Requirements.

[If the company needs to perform any site preparation work, make sure the contractor agrees in the contract that the deliverables will be

compatible with the prepared site in terms of power needs, clearances, access, or environmental (temperature, humidity) considerations. Avoid making any promises or representations regarding access or sub-surface conditions. Incorporate documents references regarding subsurface conditions following the guidelines contained under Step 7.]

13. Safety and Security Requirements.

[Specify any safety and security requirements.]

14. The Replacement Parts and Consumables.

[Specify how replacement parts or consumables will be obtained.]

15. Shipping, Packing and Labeling Requirements.

[Specify the separate shipping instructions applicable to the individual deliverables (e.g., equipment, hardware, software, data, etc.). State any applicable notification requirements you want from the supplier as well as the method (e.g., plane, rail, truck, etc.) and delivery terms (e.g., FOB destination, FOB. shipping point, etc.). Specify if there are any special packing or labeling instructions with which the contractor should comply.]

16. Training Needs for Existing and New Personnel.

[If the deliverables include training, specify the number of employees to be trained, when and where the training will take place, the duration of the training, whether it will be continuous or segmented, the nature and number of the training materials and

manuals, the qualifications of the individual(s) doing the training, and how travel or other expenses will be handled. Consider how replacement employees will be trained and whether the training may be videotaped.]

17.   Applicable Documents and Attachments to the Scope.

[Specify the applicable documents which may be provided as either part of the Scope of Work or for informational purposes only.]

18.   Applicable Codes and Standards.

[Specify the applicable codes and standards.]

19.   Applicable Permits and Licenses.

[Specify the applicable permits and licenses which may be required.]

20.   Contractor's Project Management.

[Specify the required contractor personnel, organization and resources.]

21.   Operation and Maintenance Manuals and Information.

[Specify the required operation and maintenance manuals.]

22.   As-Built Drawings or Final Designs.

[Specify the required contractor as-built drawings or final designs.]

23.   Schedule Delivery Requirements

[Specify the schedule delivery requirements.]

24.   Applicable Abbreviations and Acronyms used in the Scope.

[Specify the applicable abbreviations and acronyms used.]

25.   General and Other Requirements.

[Specify any general and other requirements including contractor's safety, startup, commissioning, turnover, testing, documentation, and quality control programs, if applicable.]

26.   List Attachments.

27.   *Continue if and as applicable.*

9. APPLYING A CHECKLIST TO YOUR FIRST DRAFT

Once you have completed your first draft of the Scope, apply a checklist to ensure that the basic elements of a first draft have been met. The list below can be tailored to your individual needs. Repeat the process for subsequent drafts of the Scope.

1.   Have you defined what is to be performed?

2.   Have you learned from and not repeated past mistakes?

3.   Have you linked payments to performance or progress?

4.   Have you developed a well-organized Table of Contents?

5.   Have you clearly specified the objectives to be achieved?

6.   Have you anticipated changes in needs or circumstances?

7.   Have you sought input from the right people at the right time?

8.   Have you specified the project plan, schedule and milestones?

9.   Have you specified where the deliverables will be performed?

10.   Have you avoided making any unintended (implied) warranties?

11.   Have you specified the standards or performance requirements?

12.   Have you specified the applicable testing or acceptance criteria?

13.   Have you avoided incorrect, inconsistent, or contradictory statements?

14.   Have you developed an order of precedence for the scope documents?

[END OF DESKTOP]

ATTACHMENT TO STEP 6 - COMMERCIAL STRATEGY / LEGAL LANDSCAPE

INTRODUCTION

The various compensation methods and contract templates containing the Company's standard commercial terms and conditions are set forth below:

WHEN TO USE PURCHASE ORDERS VS. CONTRACTS

1. For transactions for goods or services below $[XXX], a Plain PO (i.e., a purchase order that does not incorporate or reference Company terms and conditions) may be used, except as noted below.

2. For transactions for goods or services between $[XXX] and $[XXX], the appropriate Company commercial terms

97

and conditions must be referenced in the Purchase Order, except as noted below.

Note: A formal contract / agreement, regardless of value, must be issued for transactions involving:

a. multi-year commitments;
b. "new ventures" or joint purchases;
c. parties located in different countries;
d. technological or other obsolescence risk;
e. high potential for environmental impacts;
f. prototypical "first of a kind" goods or services;
g. regulatory and governmental bodies or entities;
h. high potential for consequential loss or damage;
i. valuable intellectual property rights (licenses, patents, copyrights, trade secrets);

3. For transactions for goods or services above $[XXX], a formal contract must be prepared.

4. For transactions for goods (equipment or materials) above $[XXXX], a formal agreement must be prepared.

COMPENSATION METHODS

5. It is, typically, the Company's responsibility to ensure that the optimal compensation method be used in procurement transactions. These methods include:

a. Lump Sum: The Company pays for the Work on a firm fixed price basis. This form of contract is best used when the scope of work is clear and well-defined and the purchaser wants price certainty. The lump sum Contract Price for the Work is paid in progress payments tied to specific milestones (or percent complete) which measure actual progress of the Work subject to retainage which is held until the Work is fully completed and accepted by the Company. The cost, overhead and profit for the Work is included in the Contract Price. Under this form of compensation, the Contractor assumes the risk that the cost of the Work specified in the scope will be greater than the Contract Price, but has the opportunity to complete the Work in the most efficient manner thereby increasing profitability. The Company assumes the risk that the Work could have been performed for less under a different form of compensation. There is no guarantee that the Contractor will make a profit under this form of compensation.

b. Time and Materials ("T&M"): The Company pays for the Work based upon the cost of hours worked (professional, craft or other) together with the cost of materials (which may include goods or equipment as well as consumables) used or provided in the performance of the Work, plus an amount (which may be a percentage or fixed fee) for overhead and profit. This form of contract is often used when the scope of work is not well-defined and the purchaser is willing to assume labor risk. Under this form of compensation, the Company assumes the risk that the cost of the Work specified in the Scope will be greater than the nominal Contract

Price. The Company assumes the risk that the Work could have been performed in a more efficient manner. Essentially, this is a cost reimbursement plus stipulated overhead and profit based arrangement. The reimbursable cost component should not include any hidden or undisclosed profit.

c. <u>Guaranteed Maximum Price ("GMP")</u>: The Company pays for the Work based upon either progress payments or time and materials as described above, but the contract price has a stipulated maximum dollar amount for the performance of the Work. This form of contract is used where the purchaser wants the flexibility of making payments based upon cost up to a maximum dollar amount. The cost, overhead and profit for the Work is included in the GMP. Under this form of compensation the Contractor assumes the risk that the cost of the Work will exceed the GMP. There is no guarantee that the Contractor will make a profit under this form of compensation.

d. <u>Target Price</u>: Company pays for the Work based upon reimbursement for the cost of time, materials and overheads and the Contractor has the opportunity to achieve a fixed fee as profit if the contract's objectives regarding cost and schedule are met. This type of compensation sometimes includes a dead band after which costs which exceed the Target Price are shared based upon an agreed and capped allocation (e.g., 50/50). Target Price contracts may also include a similar sharing mechanism for underruns. Under this form of compensation, both the Contractor and the Company assume a shared level of risk that the Work will cost more than the Target Price. The Contractor's profit is entirely reflected in the fixed fee component of the Target Price. There is no guarantee that the Contractor will make a profit under this form of compensation.

e. <u>Miscellaneous:</u> The Company can pay for Work in any number of ways. For example, the cost of equipment or materials can be based upon an agreed upon Unit Price with potential discounts for volume. In addition, certain costs may be reimbursable without markup (e.g., sales taxes, insurance, utilities, postage) and others may not be reimbursable at all (e.g., certain salaries, income taxes, cost, incurred due to fault or negligence) under the particular contract. In addition, a particular contract may include: (a) option pricing for Work or spare parts which the Company may elect to purchase on an as requested, as required basis for the particular transaction involved, or (b) T&M or Unit Pricing for out of scope work or extra materials.

f. <u>Pricing over the Long Term:</u> Escalation clauses tied to an index, such as one of the two "Consumer Price Indices" prepared by the Bureau of Labor Statistics, may bear absolutely no relationship to a provider's actual costs. This is because indices tend to be broad-based and made up of components that do not affect the provider's costs. Keeping the term of the agreement relatively short with the option to renew for subsequent terms if favorable pricing can be agreed upon is a better approach.

TERMS AND CONDITIONS

6.   It is the Company's responsibility to: (1) select the appropriate general specification that complements and is consistent with the strategy for the particular procurement; (2) tailor or otherwise modify the general specification as appropriate with any necessary input from subject matter experts ("SME"s), including the Legal Department; and (3) assemble all the contract documents including the appropriate general terms and conditions into a seamless integrated contract which: (a) supports the procurement objective for the transaction and (b) protects the Company commercially and financially. This includes the appropriate use of confidentiality agreements.

7.   The principal tool that procurement uses to support the procurement objectives and protect the Company commercially and financially are: (1) a clear and complete scope of work / supply, and (b) appropriate commercial terms and conditions. The contract types listed below can be used for the purposes indicated in cases where the short form terms and conditions are inadequate.

8.   Note that different templates may be used depending upon the State or Jurisdiction in which the applicable legal entity is located. Most of the provisions for each of these jurisdictions are identical except those pertaining to taxes, venue and how "Company", is defined.

TERMS AND CONDITIONS TEMPLATES – POSSIBLE EXAMPLES

Each organization should develop its own templates which might include:

9. **General Terms and Conditions for Construction.**

10. **General Terms and Conditions for General Services.**

11. **General Terms and Conditions for Consulting Services.**

12. **General Terms and Conditions for the Purchase of Equipment.**

13. **General Terms and Conditions for the Lease of Equipment.**

14. **Confidentiality / Non-Disclosure Agreements** ("NDA"s) - Such agreements should be used in any transaction or project, or potential transaction or project (e.g., in connection with requests for quotations, proposals, or information) where Company Confidential Information may be released.

    Company Confidential Information is information about the Company's business, operations, employees or external relationships (or similar information about other companies with which the Company has a business relationship) that is non-public or proprietary to the Company and which, if disclosed without proper authorization, could violate the law; cause potential harm or embarrassment to the Company, employees, customers, suppliers or other third parties with whom the Company has a relationship; or provide a potential advantage to a competitor or other third party.

Examples of Company Confidential Information include, but should not be limited to, information regarding property, facilities, equipment, systems, operations, outages, shutdowns, financing, financial results, forecasts, budgets, pricing, sensitivity analyses, studies, business strategies, research, plans and proposals, development or construction projects, licenses, contracts, current or prospective employees, customers, suppliers, business partners, litigation, regulatory applications and proceedings, mergers, acquisitions and divestitures.

IDENTIFYING HIGH RISK TRANSACTIONS

The following pose high risk to the Company and require commercial terms and conditions other than the pre-printed commercial terms and conditions on the reverse of the Company purchase order.

15. Transactions involving "new ventures" or joint purchases;
16. Transactions for prototypical "first of a kind" goods or services;
17. Transactions posing a high potential for environmental impacts;
18. Transactions involving parties located in different countries;
19. Transactions presenting technological or other obsolescence risk;

20. Transactions with regulatory and governmental bodies or entities;

21. Transactions presenting a high potential for consequential loss or damage;

22. Transactions with inexperienced / first time suppliers not previously used;

23. Transactions with long-term commitments; or,

24. Transactions where the Company cannot terminate for convenience at its option; or, where valuable intellectual property rights (licenses, patents, copyrights, trade secrets) will be created or exchanged.

[END OF DESKTOP]

ATTACHMENT TO STEP 7 - APPROVED BIDDERS LIST TEMPLATE

[DATE]

CONFIDENTIAL

To: [NAME]
             [TITLE]

From: [NAME]
             [TITLE]

Subject: **Recommended Bidders List for [CONTRACT NAME]**

Reference the attached documentation providing recommendations and supporting details for the following listing of bidders for the subject scope of work/supply:

- [CONTRACTOR/SUPPLIER NAME]
- [CONTRACTOR/SUPPLIER NAME]
- [CONTRACTOR/SUPPLIER NAME]

The estimated budget for this procurement is $[DOLLAR VALUE]

Additional security protection (i.e., letters of credit, retention and parental guarantees) may be required for bidders rated as "Non-Investment Grade" or with below average safety performance histories.

The Company will be issuing a request for proposal ("RFP") to these bidders. Acceptance of bidder proposals will be contingent upon Company completed review and acceptance of bidders' qualifications. Please refer to the attachments for further details.

Signatures: [NOTE: Approval must be at the appropriate executive level based on anticipated dollar value.]

Recommended: **Approved:**

_____   _____   _____   _____
[NAME]   Date   [NAME]   Date
[TITLE]   [TITLE]

_____   _____   _____   _____
[NAME]   Date   [NAME]   Date
[TITLE]   [TITLE]

Attachments [Attach additional documents supporting recommendation as necessary including pre-qualification questionnaire (if completed), as well as bidders' addresses and contact information.]

ATTACHMENT TO STEP 8 - CONFIDENTIAL INFORMATION

<u>Instructions for using this Desktop:</u>

Insert instructions specific to your organization's needs and requirements.

<u>CONFIDENTIALITY AGREEMENTS</u>

Confidentiality Agreements ("CA"s), also known as Non-Disclosure Agreements ("NDA"s) are a common way of protecting sensitive or proprietary information with competitive or commercial value. A CA is essentially a contract governing how the parties will treat confidential information. Although there are many thematic variations, all CAs share the same basic principles discussed below.

Consider The Situation - Negotiations Or Existing Contract.
A CA is used in two basic situations: 1) As part of negotiations toward reaching agreement or 2) as part of an existing contract or relationship. In the first situation, the parties may need to obtain confidential information to determine whether to enter into a contract (e.g., make a purchase, form

a joint venture, etc.). In the second situation, the parties may need to use confidential information in the course of performing their contract. When used in the context of an existing agreement, the confidentiality provisions are usually incorporated into the text of the agreement.

Consider What Will Be Provided - Business And / Or Trade Secrets.

There are two basic types of information that are provided in the context of a CA:

- **Business secrets** consist of information regarding plans or strategies or events in the conduct of business and can include such things as the amount or terms of a secret bid, the salary of certain employees, investments contemplated, the date and content of an announcement of a new policy or product, or the like. Business secrets typically do not need to be kept confidential as long as trade secrets.

- **Trade secrets** consist of business practices or information which provide the owner with a competitive advantage and can include such things as formulas, production data, compilations of information, technical information, processes, procedures, designs, or the like. Trade secrets can be important for decades or even longer since, unlike copyright or patents, they never expire and remain confidential as long as the information is kept secret.

CONFIDENTIALITY AGREEMENTS CHECKLIST

I. General Considerations

1. When do you need a Confidentiality Agreement?

Never, sometimes, always?
During exchanges in the course of negotiations
During exchanges in the course of an agreement

2. Why do you want a Confidentiality Agreement?

You want one
Both parties want one
The other party wants one

3. What information will be protected?

Information with a commercial value
Information affecting bargaining power
Information affecting the ability to compete

4. Do you trust the other party?

Examine the systems which are in place
Consider the ethics of the other party and recipients
The best way to keep a secret is... to keep it secret

5. How much control do you have?

Limited access
Authorized copying
Flow-down provisions

II. Risk Management Considerations

1. Which way will the information flow?

Information will be provided
Information will be received
Information will be exchanged

2. What is the nature of the protected information?

Documents or media
Oral communications
Ideas or concepts

3. Is the information valuable and, if so, to whom?

To the provider
To the recipient
To third parties

4. Who will rely on the information provided?

The recipient
Subcontractors
Other third parties

5.   What representations or conditions apply?

Express warranty
Implied warranty
Warranty disclaimer

III. Drafting Considerations

1.   What information is covered and must it be marked?

Business secrets
Trade secrets

2.   Who will be allowed access and under what conditions?

Employee of the parties
Contractors and subcontractors
Other third parties with a need to know

3.   What security measures, if any, will be required?

Those currently in place
Restrictions on copying the information
Additional security measures

4.   What is the standard of care to be used?

Reasonable efforts
Held in trust and confidence
Dishonest acts of the parties

5.   **How will intangible information be handled?**

Ideas and concepts
Verbal communications
Use of confirmatory notices

6.   **When will the agreement begin and end?**

One year
Ten years
More than ten years

7.   **What information is excluded?**

Public domain
Independently developed or already known
Obtained from third party with a right to disclose
Subpoenas or other types of governmental orders
Information not marked as confidential

8.   **What are the return / destruction obligations?**

Upon termination
Upon written request
What, when, and to where

9.   **Is there a limitation of liability clause?**

Cap on dollar amount
Exclusion of consequential damages

10. **What are the choice of law and venue provisions?**

Applicable law
Forum for litigation

11. **What restrictive covenants apply?**

Protect legitimate interests
Do not impose undue hardship
Do not impair the public interest
Are reasonable in terms of:

a)   Geographic area
b)   Period of applicability
c)   Scope of restricted activity

[END OF DESKTOP]

ATTACHMENT TO STEP 13 - PRICE ADJUSTMENTS

<u>Instructions for using this Desktop:</u>

Insert instructions specific to your organization's needs and requirements.

PRICING ADJUSTMENTS

Long-term contracts sometimes contain clauses which adjust the contract price over the course of time. The adjustment mechanisms are often called "escalation clauses". The better practice is to designate them as "adjustment clauses" since prices can be adjusted down as well as up. These clauses anticipate the effects of inflation or other factors affecting cost. Typically, this is done by tying price to some index.

Since adjustment clauses can have unintended consequences, care needs to be taken in how they are structured. If the goods or services can be purchased on a fixed or cost-plus basis, the risk of an adjustment clause can be avoided. Assuming that such pricing is not an option, the following points should be considered before agreeing to be bound by an adjustment clause:

1) Anticipate that market prices may <u>decrease</u>.
2) Secure the right to <u>terminate</u> the agreement.
3) Specify <u>how</u> price adjustments will be made.
4) Specify <u>when</u> price adjustments will be made.
5) Specify the <u>exact index</u> or part (and base year).
6) Clearly state any <u>caps or limits</u> on adjustments.
7) Review all <u>possible indices</u> which could be used.
8) Make a determination as to the <u>best index</u> to be used.
9) Ensure the index is <u>related</u> to what is being purchased.
10) Anticipate that an index <u>may change</u> or be discontinued.
11) Identify the applicable <u>base price</u> and <u>specific date</u> for same.

As noted above, an index for a particular transaction should be selected based on the type of project or procurement contemplated. Moreover, indices should be selected based on the type of cost being. For example, an escalation index for process piping would be inappropriate for use with a cost estimate for a building project.

Cost indices have limitations since they are based on average data. Thus, judgment is required in deciding if an index applies to a specific cost being updated. By carefully crafting adjustment clauses to reflect the cost increases against which the seller should be protected, the risk of a "runaway" price escalation and overpayment by the purchaser can be reduced.

Strong termination rights with the option to end the agreement on acceptable terms is another way a purchaser can protect itself against unanticipated consequences of adjustment clauses. Termination rights are especially important when there is no cap on the escalation.

Usually, only some components of a purchase drive the need for an adjustment clause. Ideally, the index used reflects only those components. Large indices are often composites which may not have any real correlation to the particular component(s) that are driving the desire for an adjustment clause. Moreover, just because an index has in the past, whether by coincidence or circumstance, had a correlation with price changes associated with a particular component, there is no guarantee that the correlation will continue. Where the price of one component has a disproportionate affect on total cost, an adjustment clause predicated on a broadly based index will not reflect actual costs.

Since such clauses are designed to protect against long-term price changes, it may not make sense to have them apply immediately. Nor should such clauses protect the supplier against avoidable costs or costs already incurred. Consider placing limits on the adjustment clause. The escalation could be made to apply only after a certain time or after costs have risen by a certain amount. It may not make sense to apply the adjustment clause or the same index to all components of a procurement. Purchases involving a combination of both goods and services may warrant that different (or no) adjustments be made to certain components.

Note that if the contract contains a Force Majeure clause excusing performance under certain circumstances, it may be appropriate to stipulate that the escalation provisions are tolled for the period of any Force Majeure.

ALTERNATIVES TO ADJUSTMENT CLAUSES

A Cost-Plus Contract is one alternative to using adjustment clauses. Be sure to clearly and completely identify which costs are included and which cost components are to be reimbursed with a fee and which at cost without mark-up. Also make sure that there are strong audit provisions in cost-plus contracts.

A Surcharge is an addition to the price based on cost increases on one component. Such a surcharge could be based on actual cost or an applicable index. Most of the considerations applicable to adjustment clauses are likewise applicable to surcharges, including how and when they are calculated and whether they reflect either price increases or decreases.

Option to Purchase is the right, but not the obligation to buy at some set price. Usually, an option requires that consideration be paid for the right to buy in addition to the price to be paid for the goods or services to be purchased. By contrast, "firm offers" to sell goods are good for three months, without the need for any financial or other consideration.

Increasing Prices are the assumption that prices will continue to rise by some arbitrary amount. Simply agreeing to progressively raise prices might not make sense, since the prices set may not necessarily reflect true cost or be competitive. Purchasers need to take the possibility of declining prices into consideration, and progressively higher pricing ignores that important aspect of a purchase. Also bear in mind that pricing can have an effect on a supplier's incentive to deliver at a particular time.

Price Upon Delivery should only be used where it can be structured in such a way that the price is determined by competitive forces and not simply set by the supplier. Most "favored nations" provisions (guaranteeing pricing will not be less favorable than that offered to other customers for similar quantities) offer some protection, but do not apply where the goods or services are designed to suit a particular purchaser's unique needs.

COMPENSATION CONCEPTS FOR MINIMIZING CHANGES IN TARGET PRICE CONTRACTS

1. The Contract Price for [PROJECT NAME] is $[_____] and consists of the Lump Sum Price of $[_____] and the Target Price of $[_____].

2. The above Contract Prices are intended to provide the Company with a high degree of budgetary certainty and reflect Contractor's commitment to achieve the Company's objectives on time and within budget. Toward that end, Contractor commits to minimize its requests for Changes under the Contract and to limit its Change Requests as specified herein.

3. For the Target Price portion of the Contract, Contractor will be compensated at full rates per Exhibit [___] up to the Target Price. Beyond the Target Price, Company will be charged at Contractor's cost without profit up to 110% of the Target Price. Beyond 110% of the Target Price, Contractor will be compensated at full rates per Exhibit [___].

4. Contractor is entitled to earn an Incentive Fee in the event the Target Price is underrun and such Target Price Underrun shall be shared between the Parties on 60/40 percent basis, with 60% of the Target Price Underrun payable to the Company.

5. Changes to the Work will only increase the Target Price where the cost for out of scope work exceeds $[___] per

occurrence and such individual occurrences, and directly related costs, are documented by a Change Order Request demonstrating an increase in such cost and a Change Order is issued by the Company.

6.   Changes to the Work will only increase the Lump Sum Price where the cost for the out of scope work exceeds $[___] per occurrence as specified in the Contract above and is documented by a Change Order Request demonstrating an increase in the Indirect Costs and a Change Order is issued by the Company.

7.   Indirect Costs means all costs related to indirect costs or expenses including construction equipment, home office support or charges, mobilization, health and safety (including the Health and Safety Plan, "HASP"), insurance and credit guarantees, and indirect labor and supervision.

ATTACHMENT TO STEP 15 - FINANCIAL RISK MANAGEMENT

1. INTRODUCTION

When hiring a contractor or supplier, there are three key factors to consider: "character, capability and creditworthiness". The term "creditworthiness" is a subjective judgment about a counter-party's financial ability to fulfill its contractual obligations. Evaluating this financial ability is essential and an important reason to select a qualified contractor with expertise and experience. One step in seeking an appropriate level of protection and predictability is to secure adequate contractual rights and remedies including the right to:

1. Terminate, suspend, or demand adequate assurances of performance.
2. Obtain status and schedule data.

3.   Increase or decrease the scope of work.

4.   Withhold payments.

5.   Set off company claims against amounts owed.

6.   Retainage.

7.   Required invoice documentation.

8.   Hold payments until due.

9.   Insurance coverage.

10.   Securing credit guarantees such as letters of credit or paren-
      tal guarantees.

Every transaction has risk and the level of that risk will depend on many factors including the amount of competition, the respective leverage the parties have and the relative need for the goods / services involved. The acceptability of a particular transaction needs to be judged holistically given all of the facts and circumstances.

2. REVIEW AND APPROVALS

The process for review and approvals regarding financial risk management are addressed in the company's commercial practices manual.

In a nutshell, if a contract is over $[_____] with a new counter party or over $[_____] with a previous counterparty the transaction requires a review by risk management specialists.

The principal tools and methods that procurement uses to protect the company from the financial risk associated with commercial transactions are set forth below. This list is designed to assist the company in making the necessary decisions or recommendations regarding how to manage the risk that the seller or contractor will not have sufficient financial strength to perform its contractual responsibilities including warranty obligations.

3. STEPS FOR ASSESSING FINANCIAL STATUS

Obtain publicly available information.
Review Dun & Bradstreet or similar reports.
For public entities obtain recent financial audits.
Evaluate whether information available suggests a risk.

4. NEGOTIATING FAVORABLE PAYMENT TERMS

Ensure proper payment cycle time period (e.g., 30 days).
Ensure proper company form of requisition of payment is used.
Ensure invoices become due only upon being properly submitted.
Ensure prompt payment discount provisions are available to the company.
Note: Be aware of various state "Prompt Payment" statutes.

5. NEGOTIATING FAVORABLE RETAINAGE TERMS

Ensure retainage (typically five (5) to ten (10) percent).
Ensure retainage is not payable until all work is fully completed.
Note: Be aware of various state statutes restricting the amount of retainage.

6. NEGOTIATING FAVORABLE OFFSET / SETOFF TERMS

Ensure the company has the right to offset / setoff against other contracts.

Ensure the company has the right to deduct for claims / backcharges / self-help / audit cost.

7. OBTAINING LETTERS OF CREDIT

Ensure letters of credit are from qualified institutions.
Ensure letters of credit are in the form supplied by the company.
Ensure letters of credit remain in effect through full warranty period.
Ensure original copy of letter of credit is filed with risk management.
Track expiration dates and ensure renewals are up-to-date.

8. OBTAINING PARENTAL GUARANTEE

Ensure parental guarantee is from actual parent company.
Ensure parental guarantee is in the form supplied by the Company.
Ideally, parental guarantee remains in effect through full warranty period.
Ensure original copy of parental guarantee is safely filed and retrievable.
Track expiration dates, if applicable.

9. OBTAINING INSURANCE COVERAGES

Obtain appropriate insurance coverages.
Track expiration dates and ensure renewals are up-to-date.
Ensure certificates are on file, consistent with contractual requirements.

10. NOTE

Payment and performance bonds should be used rarely and carefully. Where such bonds are to be used: (1) separate payment and performance bonds should be purchased, and (2) the company's form of payment and performance bonds should be obtained from the Law Department for use.

11. KEY RISKS TO CONSIDER

1. The failure to integrate market intelligence with decision making.

2. The failure to identify and assess the risks to the supply chain.

3. The failure to prioritize risks and integrate past learnings.

12. FINANCIAL RISK MANAGEMENT TOOLS

1. Letters of Credit (see attached sample template).

2. Parental Guarantees (see attached sample template).

3. Payment and Performance Bonds (see attached template).

13. BANKRUPTCY ISSUES

Bear in mind that it is very difficult to protect yourself against a supplier's bankruptcy using ordinary commercial contract language. This is why people use letters of credit and parental guarantees. It is clear that especially in the United States, bankruptcy laws protect the debtor to an extraordinary degree. However, there are practical steps you can take to mitigate the consequences of supplier bankruptcy including the steps discussed in this desktop. Aside from avoiding financially weak firms, progress payments, retainage, letters of credit, parental guarantees and surety bonds can mitigate bankruptcy risks. In addition, if goods are to be stored on the supplier's premises or under its control, the goods should be segregated behind "lock and key" with appropriate signage identifying the goods as having been bought and paid for by your firm. The goal is to clearly identify the goods as owned by your firm or "work-in-progress" and specifying that your firm can take possession of these goods and finish the manufacturing, development or distribution process. Also recall that bankruptcy laws are very technical and merit appropriate attorney involvement.

[END OF DESKTOP]

IRREVOCABLE, TRANSFERABLE, STANDBY LETTER OF CREDIT

Date: _____   Amount: $_____

Letter of Credit No.

Beneficiary: [INSERT NAME AND ADDRESS OF BENEFICIARY]

Ladies and Gentlemen:

We (the "Issuer") hereby establish our irrevocable, transferable, standby Letter of Credit No. _____ in your favor and for the account and at the request of [NAME OF APPLICANT] (the "Applicant"), whereby we irrevocably authorize you to draw on us from time-to-time at sight prior to the expiration hereof, and in the manner provided herein, up to _____ Dollars ($_____ USD). Multiple and partial drawings are permitted. Funds under this Letter of Credit will be available to you upon your presentation of a drawing certificate, executed by one of your duly authorized representatives, in the form of Attachment A, "Drawing Certificate".

Presentation may be made for payment (in immediately available funds by wire transfer to the account of the Beneficiary designated in the Drawing Certificate) at the office of Issuer located at [ADDRESS OF ISSUER] (the "Presentation Office") on any Business Day. A "Business Day" shall mean any day other than Saturday, Sunday or any day on which commercial banking institutions in [CITY IN WHICH PRESENTATION OFFICE IS LOCATED] are authorized or required by law to close.

If a Drawing Certificate is presented at the Presentation Office on or before [10:00 a.m.], _____ Time, on a Business Day, we will pay to the Beneficiary (as directed in the Drawing Certificate) the amount demanded therein in immediately available funds by wire transfer to the account of the Beneficiary designated in the Drawing Certificate, no later than [5:00 p.m.], _____ Time, on the same Business Day. If a Drawing Certificate is presented at the Presentation Office after [10:00 a.m.], _____ Time, on a Business Day, we will pay to the Beneficiary (as directed in the Drawing Certificate) the amount demanded therein in immediately available funds by wire transfer to the account of the Beneficiary designated in the Drawing Certificate, no later than [1:00 p.m.], _____ Time, on the next succeeding Business Day. Any payment made hereunder shall be made without setoff or counterclaim. The Issuer hereby waives any rights of subrogation that it may acquire at law or in equity as a result of making any payment hereunder.

Typographical errors other than in amounts are not considered discrepancies.

Faxed document(s) are acceptable.

Except as hereafter provided, this Letter of Credit shall remain in full force and effect until the 5:00 p.m. _____ Time on _____, 20__. This Letter of Credit shall be automatically renewed after _____, 20__ for successive one (1) year periods unless we provide Beneficiary with not less than sixty (60) days prior written notice that we elect not to renew this Letter of Credit.

This Letter of Credit shall be freely transferable by the Beneficiary hereunder on one or more occasions in whole, but not in part, and any such transfer shall be effective upon written notice thereof to the Issuer.

The obligation of the Issuer to make payment under this Letter of Credit is independent of, and is not conditioned upon, the payment of any fee. All fees and other costs chargeable by the Issuer in connection with this Letter of Credit are for the account of the Applicant and shall not in any manner be a liability or responsibility of the Beneficiary.

This Letter of Credit (which includes the attached Form of Drawing Certificate) sets forth in full the terms of our undertaking and such undertaking shall not in any way be modified, amended or amplified by reference to any document or instrument referred to herein, or in which this Letter of Credit is referred to, or to which this Letter of Credit relates, and no such reference shall be deemed to incorporate herein by reference any document or instrument.

This Letter of Credit is issued subject to the International Standby Practices, I.C.C. Publication 590 ("ISP98"), except to the extent that the terms hereof are inconsistent with the provisions of ISP98, including but not limited to Rule 5.01ai of ISP98, in which case the terms of this Letter of Credit shall govern, and as to matter not addressed by the ISP98 shall be governed and construed in accordance with the laws of the State / Jurisdiction and applicable U.S. Federal law.

We hereby (A) irrevocably submit to the jurisdiction of the [STATE] courts or Federal District Court in [STATE] for the purpose of any suit, action or other proceeding arising out of this Letter of Credit, and (B) to the extent permitted by law, hereby irrevocably waive, and agree not to assert, by way of motion, as a defense, or otherwise, in any such suit, action or proceeding any claim that we are not subject to the jurisdiction of the above-named courts, that suit, action or proceeding is improper or that this Letter of Credit may not be enforced in or by such court.

By:

ATTACHMENT A
FORM OF DRAWING CERTIFICATE

(DATE)

[NAME AND ADDRESS

OF ISSUER]

Attention:

Re: Irrevocable, Transferable, Standby Letter of Credit No. _____

Dated _____

Ladies and Gentlemen:

1. Any capitalized terms used and not otherwise defined herein shall have the meanings set forth in the above-referenced "Letter of Credit".

2. The undersigned certifies that the undersigned is an authorized representative of [INSERT NAME OF BENEFICIARY], the beneficiary of the Letter of Credit, and hereby further certifies as follows:

    (a) [INSERT NAME OF BENEFICIARY] is the beneficiary of the Letter of Credit (the "Beneficiary"), and hereby demands the payment of U.S. $_____ to the following account:
    [Insert wire instructions (to include name and account number of the Beneficiary)]

(b)   The amount demanded in this Drawing Certificate does not exceed the amount of the Letter of Credit on the date hereof.

(c)   Pursuant to the terms and provisions of that certain [STATE AGREEMENT BETWEEN BENEFICIARY AND APPLICANT TO WHICH THIS LETTER OF CREDIT RELATES], Beneficiary is entitled to the draw of the funds requested under this Drawing Certificate.

IN WITNESS WHEREOF, the undersigned has executed this Drawing Certificate as of the _____ day of _____, _____.

[INSERT NAME OF BENEFICIARY]

By:_____

    Name:

    Title:

PARENTAL GUARANTEE

[NAME OF GUARANTOR]

PARENTAL GUARANTEE ("Parental Guarantee")

FOR THE BENEFIT OF [_____]

1.   [NAME OF CONTRACTOR], a [_____] ("Contractor"), and [_____] ("Company"), have made and entered into a contract dated _____ ("Contract"), pursuant to which Contractor shall perform the "Work" (as defined in the Contract) at the [_____], in [_____]. The Company is entitled to this Parental Guarantee pursuant to and conditioned upon [_____], [_____] of the Contract. Without this Parental Guarantee, Company would be unwilling to enter into or perform under the Contract. The undersigned Guarantor, [_____], a [_____], is a part indirect owner of Contractor and because of this relationship Guarantor has a present, vested, pecuniary interest in Contractor and Guarantor will realize a present, direct, pecuniary benefit from the execution and consummation of the Contract by Company. The Guarantor hereby acknowledges receipt of the Contract.

2.   In consideration of the above-described present and direct pecuniary benefit to Guarantor, the Guarantor hereby absolutely, unconditionally and irrevocably guarantees to

Company the full, faithful and punctual payment, performance, discharge and observance of all of Contractor's
obligations under or in accordance with the Contract, as it
may be amended or modified, including any and all claims
the Company may have against the Contractor that arise
out of the performance or breach by the Contractor of any
provision of the Contract, (the "Guaranteed Obligations"),
irrespective of any bankruptcy, reorganization, liquidation,
moratorium, insolvency or similar proceedings affecting
Contractor. The guarantee of the Guarantor as set forth
herein is a guarantee of payment and performance and
not merely of collection and is not conditioned or contingent upon the pursuit by Company of any remedies which
Company now has or may hereafter have under the Contract,
at law, in equity or otherwise for Contractor's default in the
performance of the Guaranteed Obligations. This Parental
Guarantee shall terminate and be discharged on the date
on which all of the Guaranteed Obligations have been paid,
performed, discharged and observed. The Guarantor shall
not have the right to terminate this Parental Guarantee or
to be released, relieved or discharged from their obligations
hereunder, arising out of the performance or nonperfor-
mance of the Contract by Company or Contractor.

3.   If Contractor fails in the payment, performance, discharge
and observance of any of the Guaranteed Obligations on
or before the times such Guaranteed Obligations are to
be performed under the Contract, then Guarantor, upon
receipt of Written Notice of such failure and demand
from Company, shall assume full responsibility for the

payment, performance, discharge and observance of the Guaranteed Obligations in accordance with the Contract, and Guarantor shall be fully liable to Company thereunder. If the Guarantor fails to perform and discharge the Guaranteed Obligations hereunder and under the Contract promptly when required, Company may pursue any remedies at law or in equity against Guarantor. All such Written Notices to be given hereunder shall be effective upon receipt and shall be in writing and delivered by hand, overnight courier service, or first class mail to the Guarantor or Company, as the case may be, at the following addresses (or such other addresses as may hereafter be designated in writing):

(a)   If to [Contractor]:

*

*

*

If to [_____]:   Copy to:

[____]   [____]
                                         [____]

4.   Guarantor hereby represents and warrants to Company that:

(a)   It holds an indirect ownership interest in Contractor; and Guarantor is duly organized and validly existing and in good standing under the laws of [_____].

(b)   The execution, delivery and performance by it of this Parental Guarantee has been duly authorized by all requisite corporate action, is within its legal power and capacity and will not violate any provision of applicable law, any order of any court or agency of government or any indenture, agreement or other instrument to which it is a party or by which it is bound, or be in conflict with, result in a breach of, or constitute by itself or with due notice, the passage of time or both, a default under any such indenture, agreement or instrument.

(c)   It shall not sell, transfer, or assign its assets by operation of law or otherwise, unless the successor to such assets remains liable for all the obligations under this Parental Guarantee.

(d)   It shall not assign this Parental Guarantee without the prior written consent of the Company.

(e)   This Parental Guarantee constitutes a legal, valid and binding obligation on the part of Guarantor.

5.   In the event Guarantor shall become liable to perform any Guaranteed Obligation, then any payment made by Company pursuant to the Contract, whether to Guarantor or Contractor, shall be deemed to have been made to the appropriate party under the Contract.

6.   Guarantor agrees that the time and/or manner of payment and performance of the Guaranteed Obligations may

be modified, amended or waived in accordance with the Contract or by agreement by Contractor and Company without notice to or the consent of Guarantor. Guarantor expressly waives for itself (but not for the Contractor if required by the Contract): (a) notice of acceptance of this Parental Guarantee by Company; (b) presentment and demand for payment; (c) protest and notice of dishonor or of default; (d) any right to require Company to proceed against Contractor or to require Company to pursue any other remedy or enforce any other right in the event of Contractor's default; (e) any notice of any kind with respect to the performance or lack of performance of the Guaranteed Obligations by Contractor or of any adverse change in Contractor's condition or any other fact that might increase Guarantor's risk; and (f) all other rights, defenses and notices to which such Guarantor would otherwise be entitled.

7.   Guarantor intends that Company rely upon this Parental Guarantee, which in turn is expressly intended to be absolute, unconditional and irrevocable. Guarantor's obligations under this Parental Guarantee nor any remedy for the enforcement thereof shall be impaired, modified, changed or released in any manner whatsoever by an impairment, release, discharge or limitation of the liability of Contractor by reason of bankruptcy or insolvency, it being expressly understood and agreed that Guarantor has assumed any and all risks of Contractor's bankruptcy or insolvency.

8.   This Parental Guarantee shall be binding upon Guarantor and its successors and assigns and shall be for the benefit

of and shall be enforceable by Company and its successors. No assignment by Guarantor shall relieve Guarantor of any liability to Company. This Parental Guarantee is intended for sole benefit of Company, and there are no third party beneficiaries to, of or under this Parental Guarantee.

9. THIS PARENTAL GUARANTEE SHALL BE GOVERNED, CONSTRUED AND ENFORCED ACCORDING TO THE INTERNAL LAW OF THE STATE OF [STATE], WITHOUT REFERENCE TO THE PRINCIPLES OF CONFLICT OF LAWS. ANY CLAIM UNDER OR DISPUTE ARISING OUT OF THIS PARENTAL GUARANTEE SHALL BE SUBMITTED TO THE EXCLUSIVE JURISDICTION OF THE FEDERAL COURTS IN [STATE] OR THE COURTS OF THE STATE OF [STATE], AND GUARANTOR HEREBY SUBMITS TO THE IN PERSONAM JURISDICTION OF SUCH COURTS. THE GUARANTOR IRREVOCABLY CONSENTS TO THE SERVICE OF PROCESS OF ANY OF THE AFOREMENTIONED COURTS IN ANY SUCH ACTION OR PROCEEDING BY REGISTERED OR CERTIFIED MAIL TO THE GUARANTOR. THE GUARANTOR HEREBY IRREVOCABLY WAIVES ANY RIGHT OF TRIAL BY JURY IN ANY ACTION, PROCEEDING OR COUNTERCLAIM ARISING OUT OF OR IN CONNECTION WITH THIS PARENTAL GUARANTEE OR ANY MATTER ARISING HEREUNDER.

10.   No amendment, waiver or consent relating to this Parental Guarantee shall be effective unless it is in writing and signed by the Guarantor and the Company.

11.   This Parental Guarantee constitutes the entire and only agreement and understanding existing between the Guarantor and the Company with respect to the subject matter hereof, and there are no prior written or oral agreements, commitments, representations, communications, or understandings between the Guarantor and the Company with respect to the subject matter hereof.

The Guarantor, intending to be legally bound, has caused this Parental Guarantee to be duly executed and delivered as of the _____ day of _____. 20[_]. The signatories hereto represent that they are authorized to enter into this Parental Guarantee on behalf of the party for whom they sign.

By: _____   Name:_____

Title: _____   Date: _____

Number _____

PERFORMANCE BOND

KNOW ALL MEN BY THESE PRESENTS, That we, the undersigned [NAME OF CONTRACTOR] (called "Principal"), as Principal, and [NAME OF COMPANY PROVIDING BOND] (called "Surety"), as Surety, are held and firmly bound unto [NAME OF OBLIGEE] (called "Obligee ") in the penal sum of [DOLLAR AMOUNT OF CONTRACT LET TO CONTRACTOR] Dollars [$NUMERICAL AMOUNT] for the payment of which Principal and Surety bind themselves, jointly and severally, their legal representatives, successors, and assigns, firmly by these presents.

WHEREAS, Principal has entered into a written Contract dated [DATE OF CONTRACT / PURCHASE ORDER] with Obligee for [SPECIFY NAME OF CONTRACT AND PURCHASE ORDER NUMBER] (called "Contract"), a copy of which Contract is hereby incorporated by reference and made a part hereof as fully as if set forth herein,

NOW, THEREFORE, THE CONDITION OF THIS OBLIGATION is such that if Principal shall faithfully perform and complete the Contract and promptly reimburse the Obligee for any and all losses, damages, costs, or expenses which the Obligee sustains due to the Principal's default, then the obligations under this Bond shall be void; otherwise, the Bond shall remain in full force and effect. In the event of default, Surety shall, within fifteen (15) days of default, remedy same by, at Obligee's option, either: 1) arranging for the Contractor, with the Obligee's consent, to perform and complete the Contract; or, undertaking to perform and complete the Contract itself through its agents or general contractors acceptable to the Obligee, or, 2) pay the Obligee the cost and expense of performing and completing the contract. In addition to remedying the default, Surety shall reimburse Obligee for any and all losses, damages, costs, or expenses (including reasonable attorneys' fees) the Obligee sustains due to the Principal's default or Surety's failure to remedy same. Surety hereby waives any notice of and agrees that no changes, omissions, additions, extensions, or forbearance to the Contract, including to any plans, specifications, or other contract documents, shall in any way affect the obligations under this Bond.

No right of action shall accrue under this Bond to any person or entity other than to the Obligee, and there are no third party beneficiaries to this Bond.

Signed and sealed this _____ day of _____, 20____ by their duly authorized representatives.

For Principal: For Surety:

_____   _____
        (Signature)   (Signature)

_____   _____
    (Typed or Printed Name)   (Typed or Printed Name)

_____   _____
         (Title)   (Title)

ACKNOWLEDGMENT OF SURETY

State of _____

County of _____

City of _____

On this _____ day of _____, in the year 20_____ before me personally came _____ _____, to me known, who, being by me duly sworn, did depose and say that he/she resides in _____; that he/she is the_ _____, the corporation described in and which executed the attached instrument; that he/she knows the seal of the said corporation; that the seal affixed to the said instrument is such corporate seal; and that it was so affixed by Order of the Board of Directors of the said corporation, and that he/she signed his/her name thereto by like order.

_____

Notary Public
(Seal and Stamp)

ACKNOWLEDGMENT OF PRINCIPAL

State of _____

County of _____

City of _____

On this _____ day of _____, in the year 20_____ before me personally came _____, to me known, who, being by me duly sworn, did depose and say that he/she resides in that he/she is the _____ for _____ _____, the corporation described in and which executed the attached instrument; that he/she knows the seal of the said corporation; that the seal affixed to the said instrument is such corporate seal; and that it was so affixed by Order of the Board of Directors of the said corporation, and that he/she signed his/her name thereto by like order.

_____

Notary Public
(Seal and Stamp)

PAYMENT BOND

KNOW ALL MEN BY THESE PRESENTS, That we, the undersigned [NAME OF CONTRACTOR] (called "Principal"), as Principal, and [NAME OF COMPANY PROVIDING BOND] (called "Surety"), as Surety, are held and firmly bound unto [NAME OF OBLIGEE] (called "Obligee") in the penal sum of [DOLLAR AMOUNT OF CONTRACT LET TO CONTRACTOR] Dollars [$NUMERICAL AMOUNT] for the payment of which Principal and Surety bind themselves, jointly and severally, their legal representatives, successors, and assigns, firmly by these presents.

WHEREAS, Principal has entered into a written Contract dated [DATE OF CONTRACT / PURCHASE ORDER] with Obligee for [SPECIFY NAME OF CONTRACT AND PURCHASE ORDER NUMBER] (called "Contract"), a copy of which Contract is hereby incorporated by reference and made a part hereof as fully as if set forth herein,

NOW, THEREFORE, THE CONDITION OF THIS OBLIGATION is such that if Principal shall promptly: 1) pay all persons or entities who have furnished work, labor, materials, equipment, or services for use in the improvement, said persons and entities being third party beneficiaries to this Bond; and, 2) defend, indemnify, and save harmless Obligee against any claims, suits, costs, and damages by reason of Principal's default or failure to so do, and 3) cause the dismissal or discharge of any lien claims or liens against the Obligee or its property filed by any persons or entities for work, labor, materials, equipment, or services furnished for use in the improvement; then the obligations under this Bond shall be void; otherwise, the Bond shall remain in full force and effect. In the event of default, Surety shall, within fifteen (15) days, remedy same and shall reimburse Obligee for any losses, damages, costs, or expenses (including reasonable attorney's fees) the Obligee incurs due to Principal's default or Surety's failure to remedy same. Surety hereby waives any notice of and agrees that no changes, omissions, additions, extensions, or forbearance to the Contract, including to any plans, specifications, or other contract documents, shall in any way affect the obligations under this Bond.

Other than the right of unpaid persons or entities who have furnished work, labor, materials, equipment, or services for use in the improvement to file suit for payment, no right of action shall accrue under this Bond to any person or entity other than the Obligee.

Signed and sealed this _____ day of _____, 20_____ by their duly authorized representatives.

For Principal: For Surety:

_____   _____
            (Signature)   (Signature)

_____   _____
    (Typed or Printed Name)   (Typed or Printed Name)

_____   _____
              (Title)   (Title)

ACKNOWLEDGMENT OF SURETY

State of _____

County of _____

City of _____

On this _____ day of _____, in the year 20_____ before me personally came _____
_____, to me known, who, being by me duly sworn, did depose and say that he/she resides in _____; that he/she is the_____ _____ for _____
_____, the corporation described in and which executed the attached instrument; that he/she knows the seal of the said corporation; that the seal affixed to the said instrument is such corporate seal; and that it was so affixed by Order of the Board of Directors of the said corporation, and that he/she signed his/her name thereto by like order.

_____

Notary Public
(Seal and Stamp)

ACKNOWLEDGMENT OF PRINCIPAL

State of _____

County of _____

City of _____

On this _____ day of _____, in the year 20_____ before me personally came _____ _____, to me known, who, being by me duly sworn, did depose and say that he/she resides in that he/she is the _____ for _____, the corporation described in and which executed the attached instrument; that he/she knows the seal of the said corporation; that the seal affixed to the said instrument is such corporate seal; and that it was so affixed by Order of the Board of Directors of the said corporation, and that he/she signed his/her name thereto by like order.

_____

Notary Public
(Seal and Stamp)

ATTACHMENT TO STEP 16 – RFPS / ITBS

Requests For Proposals ("RFP"s) and Instructions to Bidders ("ITB"s)

Purchasers are in the business of obtaining offers. As you know, a contract consists of: (a) an offer, (b) acceptance, (c) supported by valuable consideration, (d) for some legal object or purpose and (e) by competent parties. Thus, obtaining offers is an indispensable and critical first step in the contracting process.

Offers empower the buyer but create no obligation unless and until accepted. Offers can best be evaluated if they are presented in a format that facilitates the company's review and decision making process. Since a proposal is nothing more than an offer, there are advantages to obtaining multiple proposals. Thus, a sound process for requesting proposals is key.

Purchasers should use the RFP and ITB forms developed as a starting point and may tailor such forms as appropriate. The instructions contained in this Desktop are intended to facilitate the purchaser's use of these forms. A list of "Do's and Don'ts" follows.

DO's

1) Review all relevant facts.
2) Determine the objectives to be achieved.
3) Specify the exact requirements or results expected.
4) Ensure alignment between objectives and client expectations.
5) Tailor request for proposal to fit specific transaction requirements.

DON'Ts

1) Blindly use past formats.
2) Fail to tailor the RFP as appropriate.
3) Overly restrict solution as part of the RFP.
4) Write the RFP before aligning with sourcing strategy.
5) Fail to adequately research and evaluate the bidders.
6) Specify conflicting or restrictive standards / requirements.
7) Have too many or generic / vague requirements.

OTHER CONSIDERATIONS

As noted above, an RFP for a particular transaction should be selected and tailored to the type of project or procurement contemplated.

For example, an RFP for a service, system or process is different from one for goods. The bidder's offer and associated solution / project plan will be based on the RFP. As such, a poorly developed RFP that does not fully understand and reflect the intricacies of the current situation and objectives to be achieved will create problems down the road. Problems may include both scope and escalating cost as well as a potentially unstable relationship between the Company and the successful bidder.

Purchasers sometimes worry more about writing the document and getting it out the door rather than on having a plan on how the RFP process will support the Company's objectives. This results in RFPs being issued before the Company fully understands its needs, knows what solution alternatives are available and sometimes even before key executives have agreed on the sourcing strategy. This unplanned approach endangers the whole sourcing process and the relationship with the bidder.

Similarly, procurements can be complex and it is therefore worth investing in a well thought out roadmap on how to achieve the benefits expected. A thorough internal evaluation of the sourcing strategy, including change management and communication planning, is always the first consideration. The RFP writing should start only after this strategy is in place.

The RFP may accurately and honestly document the existing process and the problems that exist, it should not try to fit the future solution into this box. Instead, the RFP should ask for bidders to propose their best solution (and alternative solutions) using their best practices and technology. This will allow the bidders to exhibit their flexibility, demonstrate their ability to innovate, and will typically result in a better, lower-priced solution.

A good RFP will include a responsibility matrix documenting what steps the Company wishes to retain (for approvals, controls, support and other purposes), and how the relationship will be governed. An assumption of the number of retained full-time equivalents ("FTE"s) and their skill sets should be given in the RFP. If the bidder wants to suggest any changes, they should be allowed to as part of their alternative solution.

A good RFP should only be sent to bidders once the Company has invested the proper amount of time in research, fully understands the marketplace, and has narrowed the potential matches to a select few. This level of bidder evaluation needs to be done before the RFP goes out instead of sending the RFP to dozens of bidders then trying to evaluate too many. A good shortlist number to use for the bidders to receive the RFP is four (with a couple kept in reserve in case one declines to respond). This will give the Company a good mix of potential solutions, enough time to actually read and evaluate the responses, and enough competition to drive the price down through negotiations. The lack of investment in proper research to find the right group of bidders who can fulfill the long-term needs of the company puts the whole source project in jeopardy from the start.

RFP preparation is an important first step to the evaluation of the RFPs. Bidder selection is the critical decision in the process, and special attention to this is necessary to make sure the Company ends up with the best fit. Ensure having pre-defined selection criteria (e.g., reference calls with clients of similar size and scope, review of bidder's financial strength, and site visits).

Before the RFP is written, purchasers should determine key attributes the Company is looking for in the prospective contractor / supplier as well as how the RFP will be evaluated. Depending upon the transaction, a set of questions written into the RFP that will allow the Company to evaluate responses objectively, is a powerful tool.

By having a sound RFP process, the Company can reduce its overall costs as well as improve the quality of its sourcing.

SAMPLE INSTRUCTIONS TO BIDDERS FOR WORK TO BE PERFORMED

[DATE]

[_____] (the "Company") is requesting proposals for the Work as described in the Scope of Work (SOW) documents [SPECIFY AS ATTACHED OR THE APPLICABLE DATABASE]. The bidder's response ("Proposal") to the Company's request for proposal ("RFP") must be submitted in the form of a binding bid to perform the Work in accordance with the Contract Documents.

The Work to be performed will include [PROVIDE BRIEF DESCRIPTION OF WORK TO BE PERFORMED SPECIFYING LOCATION AND PROJECT NAME].

1. Currently, the bid schedule includes the following milestone dates:

ACTIVITY	DATE
Issue Bid Event via [RFP PLATFORM]	[DATE]
Mandatory Pre-Bid Meeting at [LOCATION] Bidder must Supply Personal Protection Equipment ("PPE")	[DATE]
Deadline to Receive Bidder Questions	[DATE]
Company Target for Distribution of all Final Q&As and Issuance of any Final RFPs	[DATE]
Bids Due	[DATE]
Anticipated Award Date	[DATE]
Contractor Mobilization to [LOCATION] Jobsite	[DATE]
Overall Demobilization and Final Reports	[DATE]

2.	All Work will be contracted for as specified in the Contract Documents together with its attachments.

3.	All requests for clarifications and interpretations should be directed to the Bid Event Coordinator (via the [_____] messaging system for this event) who will coordinate responses from the Company.

[NAME]
Bid Event Coordinator
[CONTACT INFORMATION]

4.	Bidders must reply to this RFP via [_____] with your 'Intent to Bid' within three (3) business days and provide a list of names of attendees for the Pre-Bid Meeting. This acknowledgement will verify your ability to access the Bid Event via the online platform and confirm your intention to submit/not submit a proposal by the specified closing date.

5.	Bidders must submit their proposals in response to the Company's RFP in accordance with these Instructions to Bidders based on the following documents:

1)	Scope of Work
2)	Labor Rate Sheets
3)	Schedule of Values
4)	Contract Documents
5)	Equipment rental list
6)	Contract Milestone Schedule
7)	Project Control Requirements

8)   Site-Specific Special Conditions

9)   [PROJECT NAME] Construction Schedule (for information only)

10)   [OTHER]

6.   The Company's RFP and this Bid Event do not commit the Company to pay any costs incurred in the submission of the proposal, to procure or to contract for services or supplies in connection with the submission of the proposal, to pay any costs incurred in anticipation of an award, or to accept any minimum level of services or goods offered.

7.   Bidders shall carefully examine all documents accompanying the bid event, and complete all requested information as part of the bidder's proposal. The Contract Documents and SOW of this bid event will constitute, in whole or part, the basis of a Contract for performing the Work. All other information submitted in response to this bid event will be used for evaluation of the bidder's offer, but may or may not be included in any final Contract.

8.   Bidders must submit the "Proposal Pricing Input Sheet" with their bid.

9.   Bidders must submit the "Certificate of Competitive Bidding" with their bid.

10.   Exceptions to the Company's commercial terms and conditions are discouraged. However, the bidders are encouraged to submit cost saving, schedule- and labor-improving or technically advantageous alternatives and the Company,

at its discretion, may elect to consider those alternatives. The bidder shall first submit its proposal as required by the Company's request for proposal. If a bidder does not submit the requested base bid, any alternative offering cannot be accepted. If a bidder recommends any changes, deviations, substitutions, or alternatives from the documents, bidder shall describe the change fully and furnish complete information so that the Company can evaluate the alternatives. If bidder believes it would be advantageous for Company to deviate from the requirements, conditions, and provisions set forth in the bid event, then bidder may present such departures as an alternative together with the bidder's principal conforming proposal. A bidder's alternative proposal must explain in full detail the nature and extent of the proposed departure and the resultant effect on prices, schedules, quality, safety or any other aspects of the bidder's proposal. Such departures, if any, must be clearly identified and listed in a separate section of bidder's proposal that is devoted explicitly to that purpose. Considerations of any alternative proposal will be at Company's sole discretion.

11. The Company reserves the right to accept other than the lowest evaluated proposal, to accept or reject any proposal in whole or in part, and/or to reject all proposals with or without notice or reasons and, if no proposal is accepted, to abandon the Work or to have the Work performed in such other manner as the Company may elect. Partial or incomplete proposals will not be accepted.

12. Until the Bid due date, bidders may, without prejudice to bidder, modify or withdraw proposal by [Identify process

if applicable]. Bidders will no longer be able to alter any portion of their proposal after the bid event closes. If the bidder requires additional information or is in doubt as to the meaning of any part of the Contract or technical documents, bidder may submit a written request to Bid Event Coordinator for such information or clarification. For questions to be answered, they must be received at least ten (10) business days prior to the bid due date. The successful bidder shall not at any time after acceptance of its proposal make any claims whatsoever alleging insufficient data or incorrectly assumed conditions, nor shall bidder claim any misunderstanding with regard to the nature, conditions, or character of the Work to be done under the Contract. For any questions or information concerning this bid event, submit a written request to the Bid Event Coordinator thru the messaging system of the [_____].

13.   All bidders not yet registered with the Company are required to register online at [_____]. This online registration is to be completed no later than seven (7) business days after the bid event opens. The offering or receiving of gifts, entertainment, payments, loans, or other favors for the purpose of being placed on a bidders list, obtaining a contract, or favorable treatment under a contract, is prohibited. Furthermore, in the event a bidder is found to have offered or given a gratuity to obtain a contract or favorable treatment thereunder, the bidder(s) involved will be refused further bid considerations. The Company considers completely unacceptable the acquisition or use of sensitive or confidential information to which bidders or their agents are not entitled, such as

competing bidders' tender data, evaluations of proposals submitted by bidders, rankings of proposals, and so on. Bidders are required to notify the Company immediately of any solicitation or approach offering to (a) improperly disclose confidential bid information (including evaluations of bid information), or (b) improperly influence or affect the award of any contract associated with this project. Bidders are further required to notify the Company immediately if they come into possession of confidential information (including evaluations of bid information). Failure to comply with the foregoing may result in the disqualification of the bidder.

14.   Bidder shall provide a firm quotation for the Work described herein, within the time, at the rate and in the manner required, for the prices named in accordance with the Bid Event documents. Proposals are to be priced in U.S. Dollars without ties to any foreign currency conversions or escalation provisions, as shown in the Pricing section(s) for the duration of the contract period. Proposal validity period shall be a minimum of ninety (90) days after the closing date of this Bid Event.

15.   Delivery of Contractor's supply of [SPECIFY OR REFERENCE EQUIPMENT AND MATERIALS] shall be FOB Destination to Company's Project Jobsite, at [SPECIFY PRECISE PROJECT LOCATION, ADDRESS, AREA / ROOM NO.].

16.   Bidder must provide the insurance coverages listed under the Insurance article of the Terms and Conditions.

17. The submission of a proposal indicates acceptance by bidder of all conditions contained herein. During the proposal review, Company is not responsible for identifying or resolving any deviations that may be contained in bidder's proposal.

18. Should discrepancies in, or omissions from, the bid event documents be encountered, or should their intent or meaning appear unclear or ambiguous, bidder must notify the bid event Coordinator to request resolution. Replies to such notices may be made in the form of Addenda to the bid event documents, which will be issued simultaneously to all invited bidders. Bidder must acknowledge receipt of all Addenda within the proposal. Company will not be bound by, and bidder must not rely on, any oral interpretations or clarifications of the bid event documents. Such correspondence must be transmitted through the bid event Coordinator via the [_____] online platform.

19. Where applicable, a bidder may be required to sign a confidentiality agreement regarding Company-supplied sensitive information.

20. In the event a bidder decides not to submit a proposal, bidder will be removed from the bid event. Bidders are to keep bid event documents and information confidential.

21. A bidder's proposal must be submitted by a duly authorized officer of bidder's company. If bidder is a corporation, the proposal must be submitted by a duly authorized signatory officer of the corporation. The office held by the officer must be identified.

22. If a bidder submits a proposal as a partnership or joint venture, bidder must submit with its proposal, a "Power of Attorney" executed by all of the general partners or members of the joint venture. This Power of Attorney is to designate and appoint one of the general partners or members of the joint venture as a "Management Sponsor." This Power of Attorney is to authorize the Management Sponsor to submit the proposal on bidder's behalf, to act for and bind bidder in all matters relating to the proposal, and, in particular, to agree that each partner or member of the joint venture is jointly and severally liable for any and all of the duties and obligations assumed by bidder under the proposal and the contract, if awarded. The proposal must be submitted on behalf of the partnership or joint venture in its legal name by the Management Sponsor.

23. When requested by the Company, satisfactory evidence of the authority of any signatory of bidder must be furnished. The Company will only accept unified sums, rates, prices, or conditions and will not accept sums, rates, prices, or any conditions which differ between individual parties of a partnership or joint venture.

24. Bidder will provide performance security as specified.

25. The successful bidder is responsible for acquiring any and all licenses (applicable contractor's license(s), business license(s), etc.) and permits required to perform and deliver the Work (if applicable) as specified in the Scope of Work.

26.   In coordination with the Bid Event Coordinator, all technical documents and technical attachments shall only be available via [SPECIFY]. Each bidder will be issued an ID and password [SPECIFY] and may access said documents as specified.

ATTACHMENT TO STEP 22 - BID TAB

Background

Ten contractors were solicited to participate in the [XYZ] Project as set forth below:

Provided Proposal	Expressed Interest	Declined to Participate	
• [CONTRACTOR A]	• [CONTRACTOR D]	• [CONTRACTOR E]	• [CONTRACTOR H]
• [CONTRACTOR B]		• [CONTRACTOR F]	• [CONTRACTOR I]
• [CONTRACTOR C]		• [CONTRACTOR G]	• [CONTRACTOR J]

Three firms provided proposals summarized below:

Structure	Proposed By	Risk Allocation	Bid Price	Premium
	XXX		$[___]	$[___]
	YYY		$[___]	$[___]
	ZZZ		$[___]	$[___]

The proposals reflect [explain]. This makes [   ] the most favorable and economic approach on a risk adjusted basis, providing substantial savings.

The Project Team engaged in negotiations with the three above listed contractors to obtain services for the Project. The results of these negotiations are summarized below:

($M)	XXX	YYY	ZZZ	COMPANY
Estimated Project Cost				$[___]
Initial Submittal	$[___]	$[___]	$[___]	
Current Negotiated Submittal	$[___]	$[___]	$[___]	
Contract Price (including Fixed Fee)				
Initial Bids	$[___]	$[___]	$[___]	
Evaluated Bid	$[___]	$[___]	$[___]	$[___]
Hours	[___]	[___]	[___]	[___]

ATTACHMENT TO STEP 24 - WARRANTY CHECKLIST

Warranties are the heart of any agreement and merit careful consideration. Use the following checklist to ensure that all applicable rights and remedies are available as may be appropriate.

GENERAL

1. What statements or representations were made?
2. Who will be relying on such statements?
3. Will such statements be independently verified?
4. What disclaimers or limitations were placed on such statements?
5. Have all important statements been accurately recorded, documented, and incorporated?
6. Is the proposed warranty language (including limitations) consistent with the statements made?

NATURE OF PURCHASE

7. What is being purchased?

        a.   goods

        b.   services

        c.   goods and services

8.   Do special rules or conditions apply?

        a.   Statutory provisions

        b.   Choice of law and forum

        c.   Uniform Commercial Code

        d.   General common law principles

SCOPE OF WARRANTY

9.   What does the warranty cover?

IMPLIED WARRANTIES

10.   Are there any implied warranties?

        a.   implied by law

    (Services)

        1)   access

        2)   coordination

        3)   accurate information

        4)   adequate specification

        5)   financial responsibility

        6)   workmanlike performance

(Goods)

    7)   title

    8)   fitness

    9)   liens and merchantability

b.   implied by conduct

    1)   usage of trade

    2)   course of dealing

    3)   course of performance

WARRANTY TRIGGER

11.   When does the warranty begin?

    a.   upon shipment

    b.   upon installation or use

    c.   upon delivery or receipt

    d.   upon storage prior to use

    e.   upon substantial completion

WARRANTY DURATION

12.   How long does the warranty last?

    a.   for a period of time set by contract

    b.   for the applicable statute of limitations

    c.   for contracts for:

        1)   goods

        2)   services

  d.   for a certain period after discovery of breach

13.   Is the warranty period tolled during periods of repair within warranty?

14.   Is there a warranty on any repairs or replacements made under warranty?

WARRANTY REMEDIES

15.   What happens in the event of a breach?

  a.   right to reject (prior to acceptance)
  b.   repair or replacement
  c.   right to loss or damage
  d.   reperformance, if practical
  e.   right to revoke acceptance
  f.   right to consequential damages
  g.   limits, exclusions, or conditions
  h.   right to refund of all or part of purchase price

16.   What remedies are specifically excluded?

17.   What are the pre-requisites to remedies?

  a.   notice
  b.   compliance
  c.   maintenance

18. What types of damages are limited or excluded?

    a. lost profits
    b. clean-up costs
    c. replacement power
    d. third party claims
    e. loss of efficiency
    f. consequential damages

WARRANTIES APPLICABLE TO GOODS

19. What goods will be provided / incorporated into the work?

    a. equipment
    b. materials
    c. equipment and materials

20. Does the contract require such goods to be:

    a. in strict conformance with the contract?
    b. of the same type, kind, or quality specified?
    c. free from defects in:

        1) title
        2) free of liens
        3) material (proper materials used)
        4) manufacture (made as intended)
        5) workmanship (properly crafted)
        6) design (properly conceived)

d.   merchantable (implied), i.e.:

    1)   able to pass without objection in the trade

    2)   of fair average quality as described (fungible goods)

    3)   fit for their general / usual purposes of even kind, quality and quantity within the variations permitted by agreement

    4)   adequately contained, packaged, and labeled as required by the agreement

    5)   conformed to any label of affirmation of fact on the container

e.   fit for the purposes intended (implied) where:

    1)   purchaser's intent is known to seller, and;

    2)   purchaser relies on the seller's knowledge, skill, and judgment

f.   non-infringing on any patent or copyright

g.   non-violative of any proprietary interest in:

    1)   design

    2)   process

    3)   authorship

h.   able to perform as represented in:

    1)   proposals

    2)   statements

    3)   advertisements

4) promotional materials
5) samples, descriptions, photographs

i. of best (high, good) quality

j. able to provide or to be:

1) new
2) fail-safe
3) rust-free
4) good results
5) state of the art
6) readily available
7) adequately stocked
8) workable or operable
9) in good working order
10) inexpensive to maintain
11) long and reliable service
12) capable of being upgraded
13) a competent part of a system
14) as good as more expensive goods
15) capable of performing as specified
16) capable of working well as a system
17) compatible with existing equipment
18) complete in all their component parts
19) reasonably inferred from the contract
20) capable of meeting specified performance standards
21) well-suited for integration into the completed work, if to be integrated

21. When purchasing chemicals, does the seller warrant that:

    a. they have been legally manufactured

    b. they are legally available for sale and use

    c. they contain all appropriate warning labels, cautionary instructions, notices and all appropriate information regarding their use, handling, transportation, labeling, storage, and disposal

    d. all appropriate information regarding possible toxic or harmful effects and the precautionary measures to be taken to eliminate or minimize these risks has been supplied

WARRANTIES APPLICABLE TO SERVICES

22. Does the contract specify that the services, work, or design shall be:

    a. strictly (substantially) in accordance with the contract documents

    b. free from defects or faults in:

        1) design

        2) material

        3) engineering

        4) manufacture

        5) workmanship

    c. of high (highest) quality

    d. performed according to sound

1)   work practice
2)   engineering procedures
3)   technical specifications
4)   strictly (substantially) in accordance with contract documents

e.   in compliance with established industry

1)   codes
2)   standards

f.   in compliance with all applicable

1)   laws
2)   regulations, codes, and ordinances
3)   requirements of governmental authorities

g.   result in dependable service and performance

1)   as specified
2)   as can be reasonably inferred from the contract documents

h.   performed to purchaser's complete satisfaction

i.   in conformance with accepted industry standards

j.   reflective of competent (high) professional

1)   judgment
2)   knowledge

          3)   workmanship

k.   performed in an expert manner

l.   performed with a high (highest) degree of

          1)   care
          2)   skill
          3)   attention
          4)   diligence

m.   performed by individuals / entities who are

          1)   fully competent and reliable
          2)   properly qualified and licensed
          3)   properly trained and experienced
          4)   fully cooperative and trustworthy
          5)   properly organized, financed, and equipped

n.   performed in a manner which is

          1)   expert and efficient
          2)   well-supervised and controlled
          3)   well-managed and organized

o.   performed to the seller's "best efforts"

p.   performed by particular individuals

ATTACHMENT TO STEP 25 - PROPOSAL EVALUATION PRINCIPLES

INTRODUCTION

The following Evaluation Principles are intended to provide a framework for assessing bids. Accordingly, the company's evaluation of proposals shall be guided and influenced by the collective application of the following principles:

1)   Cost: Meeting all proposal requirements at the lowest cost
2)   Certainty: Providing a high degree of certainty and predictability
3)   Risk Mitigation: Reflecting the lowest risk to success
4)   Specificity: Providing a high degree of specificity and detail

Bidders must, of course, meet the minimum requirements of the bid content as specified. However, the Company shall favor bids providing the lowest cost with the highest degree of certainty and specificity as well as the lowest risk. Bidders who invest the time and effort in providing such proposals will be at an advantage. These Evaluation Principles do not affect weightings applicable specific proposals but rather are intended to provide guidance on how a company should evaluate bidders' proposals. In addition, the importance of these principles in relation to each other may vary from project to project.

COST

Company shall review proposals based on cost, which includes not only the cost to construct but the cost to operate and maintain the project. This will be an important factor in achieving the objective benefits of an economically efficient solution. Accordingly, bids achieving the objective and complying with all design requirements should receive favorable review. Bidders may also make the case in their proposals that they have gone beyond meeting design requirements and that their bid, which may exceed design requirements at greater cost, should be given favorable consideration. However, in such a case, bidders would be expected to demonstrate the added value of their design.

CERTAINTY

1. Cost. The cost of the project has a direct bearing on the project's cost / benefit ratio. Accordingly, cost certainty will be an important factor in the Company's selection decisions. Bids that provide a high degree of cost certainty shall receive more favorable review. Bidders can demonstrate cost certainty in a number of ways. For example, bidders could propose to be bound by a cost cap that would preclude recovery for costs beyond the specified binding cost cap. Likewise, bidders could explain and demonstrate their cost containment capability and the history of successfully completing similar projects / undertakings within budget.

2. Schedule. Company shall favor bids reflecting a high degree of schedule certainty as demonstrated by the quality and level of detail of the schedule of activities proposed by the bidder. Accordingly, a bidder's willingness to commit to a schedule, as well as the demonstrated ability to meet the schedule and a history of successful project completions within schedule, are important factors in the Company's evaluation. Depending upon the particular project, schedule certainty may be an especially important element of the Company's evaluation.

3. Performance. The quality of the bidder's design and the bidder's willingness to commit to the future proper operation and maintenance of the facility are important factors in the certainty of project performance. Accordingly, the degree to which the bidder demonstrates certainty that

the completed project will operate as designed, and can be operated and maintained (under normal and emergency conditions) in the manner specified and required, will impact favorably on the Company's evaluation.

RISK MITIGATION

1. Financial. Bidders providing clear and robust financial guarantees that support performance, including, but not limited to, parental guarantees, letters of credit or similar instruments will receive more favorable review.

2. Execution. Company shall evaluate the bidder's ability to successfully execute its commitments to a project based upon, among other items (as appropriate), the bidder's: (a) record and quality of its construction team, (b) demonstrated history of successful construction performance (both from a cost and a schedule perspective), (c) demonstrated positive safety record and "culture of safety", (d) ready access to staffing and workforce, (e) agreements with other parties such as strategic alliances, (f) arrangements with key suppliers and contractors, (g) ability to obtain any necessary intellectual property rights, ancillary agreements, real estate, access rights or the like, (h) applicable permitting path and status, and (i) likelihood of public support / opposition to the projects / transaction if applicable.

3. Assurance. If appropriate, the bidder's ability to demonstrate that it can meet its commitment to operate and maintain the work / facility in accordance with all requirements

over its lifespan is an important factor in the Company's evaluation. Accordingly, a bidder's ability to provide plans, protocol, and procedures to meet ordinary and emergency operations and maintenance requirements in a timely manner as well as providing a guaranteed mechanism for funding present and future operation and maintenance costs should receive favorable review. The ability to meet commitments, present and future, can be demonstrated in a number of ways including: (a) history of performance with similar facilities, (b) arrangements with local owners or contractors, and (c) establishment of a mechanism to fund present and future operations and maintenance.

SPECIFICITY

1. Design. Bidders providing greater levels of detail for cost and design beyond the minimum bid requirements will be accorded a more favorable assessment in the Company's evaluation.

2. Project Plan. Bidders providing greater levels of detail for project implementation plans beyond the minimum bid requirements will be accorded a more favorable assessment in the Company's evaluation.

3. O&M Plan. Bidders providing greater levels of detail for the project's operation and maintenance plan, if appropriate, beyond the minimum bid requirements will be accorded a more favorable assessment in the Company's evaluation.

ATTACHMENT TO STEP 26 - LETTER OF RECOMMENDATION

[DATE]

CONFIDENTIAL

To: [Vice President]

From: [Director]

Subject: **Recommendation for Award for [XYZ] Project**

The Project Team has performed a technical and commercial evaluation of bids for [_____] in connection with the [XYZ] Project as set forth below.

1. Recommendation

Based on the evaluation of competitive proposals and for the reasons stated in this Letter of Recommendation (LOR) the Project Team recommends that the [   ] Contract be awarded to [CONTRACTOR] as a time and material (T&M) reimbursable contract for the nominal Contract Price of $[XXX] with a budgeted amount of $[XXX] as described in further detail below.

As noted above, this work will be budgeted for $[XXX] including the negotiated Contract Price of $[XXX] for the base Scope of Work and a budget allowance of $[XXX] for services related to additional scope items. This approach provides the most economic risk adjusted project execution strategy to support the viability of the [XYZ] Project.

2. <u>Executive Summary</u>

Proposals from [CONTRACTORS] were evaluated by the Project Team. [CONTRACTOR A] provided the most complete and commercially / technically acceptable proposal. [CONTRACTOR A] accepted all the Company's commercial terms and conditions and equipment pricing format that will provide the Company with the most economical means to satisfy the [_____] Scope requirements.

As full consideration to the Contractor for the full and complete performance of the Work and all costs incurred in connection therewith, the Company will pay the Contractor the price of [SPELL OUT] and 00/100 dollars ($NUMERIC VALUE) (the "Contract Price"), which Contract Price is subject to revision as set forth in the Contract but cannot be exceeded without the prior written consent of the Company in the form of a Change Order.

This Contract shall be administered by [_____] or such other entity as designated by the Company (the "Contract Administrator") for and on behalf of the Company and Contractor has agreed to comply with Contract Administrator's instructions pertaining to Contractor's performance of this Contract. However, the Contract reflects that the Contract Administrator is not authorized to enter into any contractual or other commitments on behalf of the Company or to modify, suspend, terminate or otherwise change in any manner this Contract or any other contract between the Company and the Contractor. The Contract Administrator will bring any issues to the Company's attention and provide recommendations and proposed solutions for the Company's consideration.

Any change orders must be signed by a duly authorized Company employee in order to be effective. However, in the event of an emergency which could involve bodily injury or damage to Company property, Contract Administrator is authorized to direct the Contractor to perform out of scope work. The Company shall at all times have the right to change the Contract Administrator.

3. Safety [FOR WORK ON COMPANY PREMISES]

[CONTRACTOR A] has agreed to institute a comprehensive safety program which complies with all the Company's safety requirements and to provide a full time safety representative for all on-site work. The Contractor will likewise require all its Subcontractors to meet the minimum requirements of the Contractor's safety program. The Contractor has contractually committed to a dedicated safety effort with emphasis on recognition and process improvement, including monthly safety awards conferred on any site employee or subcontractor for exceptional performance in areas such as:

    a.   Housekeeping
    b.   Hazard recognition
    c.   Near miss identification
    d.   Safe work plan preparation

Awards may include milestone team lunches and individual prizes at Contractor's expense.

4. Budget

The total amount requested to fund the budget line item for the services is $[XXX]. The funding dollars include services as noted below ($[XXX]), estimated state sales tax ($[XXX]) and a [__] ([__]) percent management reserve ($[XXX]).

The above funding request reflects $[XXX] for known risks consisting of: [____]. In addition, $[XXX] has been set aside as contingency for unknown risks.

As noted above, the Contract Price for the Work is $[XXX] and includes all [STATE] sales and use tax.

To the extent the Equipment or materials furnished hereunder may be exempt from taxation under [STATE] Sales and Use Tax Law, the Company will issue the necessary exemption certificates.

In no event will the Company be responsible for or reimburse the Contractor or any of its Subcontractors for any corporate franchise, net income, import duty, or similar taxes imposed upon Contractor, including Subcontractors, for the general privilege of conducting business.

5. Schedule

[_____] will be performed within an 8 hour day, Monday through Friday with some work performed during off hours as directed by construction management. Service to commence on or before about [_____], 20[__] and continue through [____], 20[__].

6. Scope of Work / Supply

The scope of work for [_____] consists of [_____].

7. <u>Background of Bidder Selection</u>

The bid package was issued to five (5) pre-qualified contractors. [XX] contractors declined to bid. Of the remaining bidders [CONTRACTOR A] provided the most responsive and economical bid as reflected in the bid tab below:

Bidder	Base Price	Evaluated Price	Difference
[CONTRACTOR A]	$[____]	$[____]	Base
Brand X Supply Company	$[____]	$[____]	$[____]
Smith and Jones	$[____]	$[____]	$[____]
Ajax Supply Company	$[____]	$[____]	$[____]

8. <u>Commercial</u>

As noted above, [CONTRACTOR A] has agreed to commercial terms and conditions that protect the Company's interests, including taking no exceptions to the Company's commercial terms and conditions. The Contract contains a limitation of liability clause which limits the Company's liability to the Contract Price and excludes any liabilities for consequential damages.

The Contract [does/does not] contain any liquidated damage provisions [EXPLAIN]. However, the Company has the right to withhold ten (10) percent retention from each payment due. In addition, the Contractor's obligations are supported by a Parent Guarantee and Letter of Credit in the amount of twenty (20) percent of the Contract Price. The Contract contains a [__] month warranty. These favorable terms reflect competitive bidding and negotiation with bidders who were aggressively pursuing the Company's business. The net result was a [cost avoidance / cost savings] of $[___], calculated as follows: [_____]. It is anticipated that, if approved, the target date for the Contract signature will be [_____] with a [start / notice to proceed] date of [____].

9. Conclusion

The Project is seeking Management approval to award this work to [CONTRACTOR A]. [CONTRACTOR A] has the necessary experience and expertise and can perform this work in a cost effective manner that supports the objective of the Project. Accordingly, the Project requests approval for a contract award amount of $[_____] to perform the [_____].

10. Signatures

Recommended: **Approved:**

_____	_____	_____	_____
[Name]	Date	[Name]	Date
_____	_____	_____	_____
[Name]	Date	[Name]	Date
_____	_____	_____	_____
[Name]	Date	[Name]	Date

ATTACHMENT TO STEP 30 - RED-FLAGS CHECKLIST

All seasoned professionals, regardless of experience or knowledge, must be on constant guard against "red flags" in drafting and managing transactions. The list below reflects some of the possible questions to be asked to identify areas of potential risk. The preparation and use of a Contract Management Plan ("CMP") is highly recommended.

1. Is payment tied to performance?
2. Is there a CMP and who owns it?
3. Is the Scope of Work clear and complete?
4. Have the risks been identified and assessed?
5. Has confidential information been protected?
6. Are there clear lines of authority and responsibility?
7. Have key assumptions or information been verified?
8. Are there appropriate change management safeguards?
9. Have all documents incorporated by reference been carefully read?
10. Have all important representations been incorporated into the contract?
11. Are there well-understood remedies for breach or other non-performance?
12. Does the contract contain "automatic renewals" which need to be managed?

Essentially, the questions to ask stem from the acts or omissions which raise concerns regarding risks including, but not limited to, the failure to identify and assess risks, using proposals instead of well-crafted work scopes, issuing letters of intent instead of well-crafted contracts, sealing deals with a handshake, use of inappropriate phases or jargon, inappropriate "volunteering" instead of allowing the contractor to perform, interfering with a contractor's subcontractors, or dealing with financially troubled or thinly capitalized entities without the proper safeguards.

ATTACHMENT TO STEP 34 – TRANSACTION ABSTRACT

(see attached)

1. Scope of Supply/Work: [SHORT DESCRIPTION]		2. Contract Number: [XXX NUMBER]	3. Current Date: [DATE]
4. Selected Supplier (Supplier legal name and address):	6. No. Bids Solicited: [ ]	10. Supplier Contact Information: (provide to Procurement Administration for entry into the Emergency Contact List Database)	
	7. No. Bids Rec'd: [ ]		
	8. Lowest Eval'd Cost: Yes ☐ No ☐ (if no, explain in Item 11 below)	10a. Sales/Account Manager: Name: Office Phone: Mobile:	
5. Procurement Contact: Name: Office Phone: Mobile Phone:	9. Procurement Strategy: a. Competitive Bid Using: Conventional RFP ☐ or Auction ☐; OR b. Single/Sole Source ☐ (if Single / Sole Source, obtain Non-Competitive Bid Waiver form from Client)	Email: 10b. Field Service 24 hr: Emergency Phone: 10c. Executive Sponsor: Name: Office Phone: Mobile: Email:	

11. Overview of Contract

[Provide summary description of the material or services being purchased and for what location and project the Contract applies. If other than lowest evaluated cost is selected, a detailed explanation is to be provided here.]

12. Schedule

[For service contracts identify start, completion and key milestone dates. For material contracts identify delivery dates and key milestone dates.]

13. Contract Strategy

[Identify Contract type such as lump sum, cost plus, unit price, target price, etc. and rationale for selection.]

14. Payment Terms and Basis of Payment

[Identify key payment terms (i.e., Net 30) and requirements, including payment basis such as milestone complete, percent complete, work complete (Unit Price), actual cost (T&M and Cost Plus), invoice frequency (e.g.,. weekly, bi-weekly, monthly), retainage (if any), etc.]

15. Critical Action Dates

[Identify dates where the Company or Supplier is required to take action and the absence of such action would prejudice the Company's rights under the Contract or increase the Company's risk. For example, if the Contract requires the Supplier to renew a letter of credit (LOC) by date certain and the Supplier fails to do so, the Company has the right to draw on the LOC prior to its expiration date. If the LOC expires, the Company misses its opportunity to draw on the LOC and may not have the benefit of the LOC if the Supplier fails to renew it. Insurance renewals are another example.]

123

16. General terms and conditions

[Identify terms and conditions used and key exceptions or changes. At a minimum, key terms such as Warranty, Limitation of Liability, Indemnification, Liquidated Damages and Performance Guarantees must be addressed.]

17. Cost Savings

[Identify any cost savings and provide factual basis for same.]

18. Security

[Identify the means by which the Supplier's performance under the Contract is secured including Parent Guarantees, Letters of Credit, or other means.]

19. Other

[Identify any other noteworthy Contract attributes, including those resulting from the subject matter expert review identified in Item 20, below.]

20. Transaction Review Summary

A. Has Legal review been performed?   Yes ☐ No ☐
B. Has Financial Risk Management review been performed?   Yes ☐ No ☐
C. Has Accounting review been performed?   Yes ☐ No ☐
D. Has Tax review been performed?   Yes ☐ No ☐
E. Has Business Unit Finance review been performed?   Yes ☐ No ☐
F. Has Treasury Dept. review been performed?   Yes ☐ No ☐

This document is complete and accurately reflects the negotiated Contract referenced above.

Prepared by: **Reviewed by:**

_____   _____   _____   _____
[Name] / [Initials]   Date   [Name] / [Initials]   Date

                                                  _____   _____
                                                  [Name] / [Initials]   Date

                                                  _____   _____

124

193

ATTACHMENT TO STEP 37 - REJECTION LETTER TEMPLATE

[DATE]

[CONTRACTOR/SUPPLIER NAME]
[ADDRESS]
Attention: [SUPPLIER REP. TITLE]

RE: [PROJECT NAME] - **Request for Proposal; [RFP TITLE]**

Dear [NAME],

Thank you for participating in the Company's Request for Proposal (RFP) process in connection with the above referenced [PROJECT NAME].

The proposal package submitted by your firm has been evaluated by the Company and it has been decided not to accept your proposal. We very much appreciate your participation in the Company's Request for Proposal process and look forward to the possibility of working with your firm at some point in the future.

Thank you again for participating.

Sincerely,

[BUYER NAME]
[TITLE]
[PROJECT NAME]

ATTACHMENT TO STEP 38 - CHANGE MANAGEMENT PROCESS

INTRODUCTION

The process for dealing with changes and claims is addressed in the Company's commercial terms and conditions. In following the change management process set forth in the applicable Contract, the company should be mindful of the concepts and questions which follow and seek appropriate guidance from technical, legal and management experts.

CHANGE MANAGEMENT

Changes and the consequences of changes can be minimized by the following:

1. Start with a clear and complete scope of work.
2. Preserve the right to increase, modify or delete scope.

3.   Specify the price / credit for extra or deleted work.

4.   Define the requirements for changes:

     a.   Written notice

     b.   Contract change request form

     c.   Timely submittal of supporting documentation

5.   Designate single point of contact (commercial / technical) for each party.

6.   Provide notice of breach or deficient performance and request corrective action.

7.   Follow up to ensure correction or application of self-help remedy, as appropriate.

8.   Consult with subject matter experts and keep management apprised.

9.   Document all important discussions and decisions.

10.   Apply lessons learned from previous transactions.

ASSERTING WARRANTY CLAIMS

Warranty claims raise questions which the Company should address including:

1.   What is the warranty's scope?

2.   When does the warranty expire?

3.   Was there a breach of warranty?

4.   What is the value of the warranty work to be performed?

5.   Was notice provided as required?

6.   When does the remedy need to take place / be done?

7.   What remedy applies to repaired or re-performed work?

8.   How will the remedy affect cost / schedule or other work?

9. Does the contract permit "self-help" as a remedy and if so under what circumstances?

10. Have we consulted with subject matter experts and kept management apprised?

11. Have we documented all important discussions and decisions?

CLAIMS FOR EXTRAS

Claims for extras raise questions which the Company should address including:

1. Was "extra" work performed?
2. Was "extra" work authorized?
3. Was notice provided as required?
4. Are the charges properly documented?
5. Will the "extra" work affect the schedule?
6. Was the "extra" work due to error or inefficiency?
7. Are the "extra" charges consistent with the contract?
8. Are certain charges barred by the contract terms?
9. Have we consulted with subject matter experts and kept management apprised?
10. Have we documented all important discussions and decisions?

I. DELAY CLAIMS

Delay claims raise the following questions which the Company should address including:

1. Did a delay occur?
2. What/who caused the delay?
3. How does the contract allocate risk of delay?
4. Was there compliance with the notice requirements?
5. Has supporting documentation been provided?
6. Could the delay have been avoided / mitigated?
7. Are the alleged damages correctly calculated?
8. Are the alleged damages barred by the contract?
9. Have we consulted with subject matter experts and kept management apprised?
10. Have we documented all important discussions and decisions?

CHANGE MANAGEMENT PROCESS

A robust change management system is the vehicle for achieving the benefits of a good contract and sound scope of work. The benefits of such a system include: (a) absolute control of the change process, (b) real time tracking, (c) clear and accurate recordkeeping, and (d) the ability to manage commercial transactions collaboratively with far fewer personnel.

The change management process can begin in one of two ways. Either: (a) the contractor requests a change via a Change Request Form (CRF) or (b) the company issues a Change Order (CO). This is designed to ensure that the only way changes can be initiated by a contractor is to use the CRF and a good system should not allow any modifications of this form by the contractor. There should be deadlines by which the form and supporting information must be provided in order for a claim to be legitimate.

The system dictates what supporting information must be provided by the contractor on the CRF in specified fields and also tracks the status of the individual approvals by the company. Each CRF should require the approval of a specified number of company representatives. Once a CRF is accepted by the company it becomes a CO. The company can likewise reject in its discretion CRFs as inconsistent with the contract or otherwise unacceptable. By contrast, the company's supply chain professionals can issue COs to the contractor, consistent with the terms of the contract (for example, increasing or decreasing the scope of work), with or without the contractor's acquiescence.

The system should have the ability to identify in real time the status of all pending CRFs as well as generate reports regarding all COs including by number, cost and status. The advantages of such a system is that it can provide a predicable process avoiding "lost" or "misplaced" claims and associated administrative costs and delays. It can also permit the company to know where in the approval / denial process the CRF stands.

Fundamentally, a sound change management system should be able to identify who is entering the request / data (company or contractor) as well as which project or transaction is involved and then track the progress of any requests for changes and report on the status of all changes, both pending and approved.

See attached Change Management and Change Order sample forms.

[END OF DESKTOP]

CHANGE REQUEST FORM

[DATE]

Gentlemen:

The following, including the attached supporting documentation, is a Change Request for a Change under the [INSERT TITLE OF CONTRACT] between [COMPANY] and [Contractor name] (the "Contract"). Capitalized terms used herein and not defined are defined in the Contract.

Change Request No.:

Description of Change Requested:

_____

_____

_____

_____

Effect of this Change on the Contractor's Level 1 Baseline Project Schedule and Level 3 Project Schedule (If none, so state. If any, attach supporting detail):

_____

_____

_____

_____

Effect of this Change on the Work and any deadlines or milestones (If none, so state. If any, attach supporting detail):

_____

_____

_____

_____

Effect of this Change on the warranty or guarantees (If none, so state. If any, attach supporting detail):

_____

_____

_____

_____

Effect of this Change on the Contract Price (If none, so state. If any, attach supporting detail):

_____

_____

_____

_____

[CONTRACTOR]

By:
Name:
Title:
Date:

CHANGE ORDER FORM

<table>
<tr><td colspan="3"></td></tr>
<tr><td colspan="3" align="center">**[COMPANY]**
CHANGE ORDER</td></tr>
</table>

Page 1 of 1

Change Order No: _____   **Change Order Date:** _____

Reference is made to the Contract For [*description of work*] For by and between [COMPANY] (the "Company"), and [CONTRACTOR], (the "Contractor"), dated as of [*mm/dd/yy*], as amended as of the date hereof (the "Contract"). Capitalized terms not otherwise defined in this Change Order have the meanings as specified in the Contract.

Summary Description: _____

Item	Description	Cost

Contract Price Change Summary

Original Value:

Previous Approved Change Orders:

Previous Value:

Amount of this Change Order:

Current Value:

[CONTRACTOR]

By: _____

Name: _____

Title:

[COMPANY]

By: _____

Name: _____

Title:

The Contract, except as specifically amended by this Change Order, remains in full force and effect and is hereby in all respects ratified and confirmed. The execution, delivery and effectiveness of this Change Order shall not, except as expressly provided herein, operate as a waiver of any right, power or remedy of the Company under the Contract, nor constitute a waiver of any provision of the Contract. This Change Order shall be governed by, and construed in accordance with, the laws of the State of [SPECIFY STATE].

ATTACHMENT TO STEP 39 - KICKOFF MEETING CHECKLIST TOOL

(see attached)

Contractor: _____

No.	Description (if applicable)	Required	Received Date	Responsible Party
1	Executed Contract			
2	Insurance Certificate with proper coverage, verbiage, and 30 day cancellation notice			
3	Safety Plan			
4	Safety Supervisor Resumes Approved			
5	Safety Supervisor Interviewed & Approved			
6	Safety Orientation			
7	Business Licenses			
8	Emergency Numbers			
9	Quality Control Plan			
10	Project Execution Plan			
11	Contract Performance Security (e.g., LOC, PG, etc.)			
12	Medical Records			
13	Organization Chart			
14	MSDS Sheets for initial activities			
15	Employee Training Certificates			
16	Company Supplied Permits			
17	Contractor Supplied Permits			
18	National Maintenance Agreement Permission			
19	Contractor acknowledges Quality Assurance			
20	Pre-construction Conference with Building Trades			
21	Schedule(s)			
22	Review Payment Process / Procedures			
23	Environmental Compliance Plan			
24	Review of RFI Process			

(Use additional sheets if necessary)

_____   Date: _____

Project Manager

_____   Date: _____

Contracts Administrator

ATTACHMENT TO STEP 41 - CLAIMS LETTER TEMPLATES

(see attached)

[*Date*]   Letter No.: [   ]

Via email and overnight mail

[*Name*]
[*Title*]
[*Contractor / Seller Company*]
[*Street Address*]
[*City, State Zip*]

[WARRANTY NOTIFICATION / CLAIM: *Reference Contract / Agreement, as appropriate]*

INSTRUCTION: THIS TEMPLATE DESCRIBES A SITUATION WHERE THE COMPANY IS ENTITLED TO A WARRANTY REMEDY. APPROPRIATELY TAILORED, THIS TEMPLATE CAN BE USED TO PLACE THE CONTRACTOR / SELLER ON NOTICE OF A BREACH AND TO FOLLOW UP WITH THE APPROPRIATE DOLLAR CALCULATION WHEN DAMAGES ARE KNOWN. NOTE THAT THE EXAMPLES WHICH FOLLOW ARE INTENDED TO PROVIDE A GENERAL, CONCEPTUAL APPROACH AND SHOULD NOT BE USED AS A VERBATIM TEXT. INDIVIDUAL LETTERS WILL NEED TO BE WRITTEN AND TAILORED TO THE SPECIFIC SITUATION GIVEN THE PARTICULAR FACTS AND CONTRACT TERMS.

Dear [*Name*]:

Please be advised that certain [WORK/MATERIALS] provided by [CONTRACTOR / SELLER] failed to conform to the requirements set forth in the above referenced contract. The Company has discovered that the following [WORK / MATERIALS] is defective:

Specifically, (*describe the nature of the defective Work or Materials, citing the appropriate provisions of the Contract/Agreement which may include terms and conditions, Scope of Work, schedule or other contract documents as appropriate*).

Example 1: Non-Conforming Work - Inspection of the Work has revealed that the [WORK / MATERIALS] which were [PROVIDED / INSTALLED] by your firm were improperly [PERFORMED / DELIVERED / PROVIDED] in a manner inconsistent with your contractual obligations under the applicable Scope of Work and Technical Specifications. (*Describe in detail*).] Specifically, see (*cite reference, standard, or text as appropriate*). Your firm's failure to perform the Work as required by the Contract constitutes a breach of your firm's obligations under our agreement with resulting damages to the Company.

Example 2: Non-Conforming Materials - Inspection of the Work has revealed that the Materials (*specify*) installed by your firm were inconsistent with and did not comply with the contractual obligations under the applicable Scope of Work and Technical Specifications. Specifically, see (*cite reference, standard, or text as appropriate*). Your firm's failure to provide the Materials as required by the Contract constitutes a breach of your firm's obligations under our agreement with resulting damages to the Company.

Example 3: Non-Performing Work / Materials -Inspection of the [WORK / MATERIALS] has revealed that the [WORK / MATERIALS] [PROVIDED / INSTALLED] by your firm has failed to perform as promised in accordance with the contractual provisions under the applicable Scope of Work and Technical Specifications of the Contract. Specifically, see (*cite reference, standard, or text as appropriate*). The failure of the [WORK / MATERIALS] to perform as required by the Contract constitutes a breach of your firm's obligations under our agreement with resulting damages to the Company.

Example 4: Non-Performance by Contractor / Seller – [CONTRACTOR / SELLER] has failed to [COMPLETE WORK / PROVIDE MATERIALS] in accordance with the schedule required by the Company or furnish sufficient workers of the required skill, or materials of the required quality or quantity. Company has the option to supply workers, materials, or both, and do the work. Accordingly, the Company will deduct expenses incurred in engaging other contractors, and supplying workers and material from payments due or which may become due to the Contractor. If expenses exceed the balance due or which becomes due to the Contractor, the Contractor shall pay the excess to the Company.

Accordingly, the Company hereby:

For Warranty Notification / Claim where Company wants Contractor / Seller to correct non-conformance: places [CONTRACTOR / SELLER] on notice of the above-referenced defective [WORK / MATERIALS] and requires [CONTRACTOR / SELLER] to (1) immediately acknowledge it's Warranty obligations; (2) take timely and proper steps to correct the situation including, but not limited to (*specify as appropriate*); (3) keep Company apprised of all actions and steps [CONTRACTOR / SELLER] intends to take and on what schedule and; (4) complete all Warranty work on or before (*specify date*).

For Warranty Notification / Claim where Company wants to correct non-conformance itself: places [CONTRACTOR / SELLER] on notice that, due to the urgent nature of the situation, the Company intends to take all necessary corrective action at [CONTRACTOR'S / SELLER'S] expense. (*Follow up with subsequent communication once all costs have been calculated, including any markup to cover Company's indirect, administrative or overhead costs*).

The Company reserves all of its rights and remedies as provided in the Contract.

If you have any questions, please contact [*me*] at [*phone number and email address*].

Sincerely,

[*Name of Signatory*]   C: [*Project Director Name*]
[*Title of Signatory*]   [*Project Manager Name*]
                                                               [*Other as appropriate*]

[*Attachment(s), if applicable*]

[*Date*]   Letter No.: [   ]

Via email and overnight mail

[*Name*]
[*Title*]
[*Contractor / Seller Company*]
[*Street Address*]
[*City, State*] [*Zip*]

[**BACKCHARGE / CREDIT NOTIFICATION:** *Reference Contract / Agreement, as appropriate*]

INSTRUCTION: THIS TEMPLATE ADDRESSES SITUATIONS WHERE THE COMPANY IS ENTITLED TO RECEIVE A BACKCHARGE OR CREDIT. APPROPRIATELY TAILORED, THIS TEMPLATE CAN BE USED TO PLACE THE CONTRACTOR / SELLER ON NOTICE OF A BACKCHARGE / CREDIT AND TO FOLLOW UP WITH THE APPROPRIATE DOLLAR CALCULATION WHEN KNOWN. NOTE THAT THE EXAMPLES WHICH FOLLOW ARE INTENDED TO PROVIDE A GENERAL, CONCEPTUAL APPROACH AND SHOULD NOT BE USED AS A VERBATIM TEXT. INDIVIDUAL LETTERS WILL NEED TO BE WRITTEN AND TAILORED TO THE SPECIFIC SITUATION GIVEN THE PARTICULAR FACTS AND CONTRACT TERMS.

Dear [*Name*]:

Please be advised that in accordance with the terms and conditions of the above referenced Contract, the Company is entitled to a [BACKCHARGE / CREDIT] as set forth herein.

Specifically, *(describe the nature of the: (a) defective Work or Materials, citing the appropriate provisions of the Contract which may include terms and conditions, Scope of Work, schedule or other contract documents as appropriate, or (b) the Work or Materials to be deleted from Contractor's / Seller's Scope of Work / Scope of Supply.)*

Example 1: Non-Conforming Work -Inspection of the Work has revealed that the [WORK / MATERIALS] which were [PROVIDED / INSTALLED] by your firm were improperly [PERFORMED /DELIVERED / PROVIDED] in a manner inconsistent with your contractual obligations under the applicable Scope of Work and Technical Specifications. *(Describe in detail)*. Specifically, see *(cite reference, standard, or text as appropriate)*. Your firm's failure to perform the Work as required by the Contract constitutes a breach of your firm's obligations under our agreement with resulting damages to the Company. The Company corrected the non-conformity at its expense and [CONTRACTOR / SELLER] is liable for all Company costs incurred.

Example 2: Non-Conforming Materials - Inspection of the Materials provided by your firm has revealed that they were inconsistent with and did not comply with the contractual obligations under the applicable Scope of Supply and Technical Specifications. Specifically see *(cite reference, standard, or text as appropriate)*. Your firm's failure to provide the Materials as required by the Contract constitutes a breach of your firm's obligations under our agreement with resulting damages to the Company. The Company corrected the non-conformity at its expense and [CONTRACTOR / SELLER] is liable for all Company costs incurred.

Example 3: Non-Performing Work / Materials - Inspection of the [WORK / MATERIALS] has revealed that the [WORK / MATERIALS] [PROVIDED / INSTALLED] by your firm has failed to perform as promised in accordance with the contractual provisions under the applicable

Scope of Work and Technical Specifications of the Contract. Specifically, see (*cite reference, standard, or text as appropriate*). The failure of the [WORK / MATERIALS] to perform as required by the Contract constitutes a breach of your firm's obligations under our agreement with resulting damages to the Company. The Company corrected the non-conformity at its expense and [CONTRACTOR / SELLER] is liable for all Company costs incurred.

Example 4: *Non-Performance by Contractor / Seller* – [CONTRACTOR / SELLER] has failed to [COMPLETE WORK / PROVIDE MATERIALS] in accordance with the schedule required by the Company or furnish sufficient workers of the required skill, or materials of the required quality or quantity. Company has the option to supply workers, materials, or both, and do the work. Accordingly, the Company will deduct expenses incurred in engaging other contractors, and supplying workers and material from payments due or which may become due to the Contractor. If expenses exceed the balance due or which becomes due to the Contractor, the Contractor shall pay the excess to the Company. The Company corrected the non-conformity at its expense and the [CONTRACTOR / SELLER] is liable for all Company costs incurred.

Example 5: *Scope of Work / Supply Deleted / Reduced* – Pursuant to the terms and conditions of the Contract (*cite specific Article*), the Company has elected to reduce your firm's [SOW /SOS]. Specifically, (*describe the reduction and include a revised SOW / SOS together with Change Order, if and as appropriate*).

Accordingly, the Company hereby:

notifies [CONTRACTOR / SELLER] that it is liable to the Company in the amount of ($_____) due to the [BACKCHARGES / CREDITS] described above. The Company will credit the Contract Price in this amount to cover the cost of the [BACKCHARGE / DELETED SOW/SOS]. This amount reflects all the Company's costs associated with the [BACKCHARGE / CREDIT]. [CONTRACTOR / SELLER] warranty obligation remains in full effect on Work performed and Materials provided.

The Company reserves all of its rights and remedies as provided in the Contract.

If you have any questions, please contact [*me*] at [*phone number and email address*].

Sincerely,

[*Name of Signatory*]   C: [*Project Director Name*]

[*Title of Signatory*]   [*Project Manager Name*]

                                                                 [*Other as appropriate*]

[*Attachment(s), if applicable*]

[*Date*]   Letter No.: [   ]

Via email and overnight mail

[*Name*]
[*Title*]
[*Contractor / Seller Company*]
[*Street Address*]
[*City, State*] [*Zip*]

[**RESPONSE TO CONTRACTOR / SELLER CLAIM:** *Reference Contract, as appropriate*]

INSTRUCTION: THIS TEMPLATE ADDRESSES SITUATIONS WHERE THE COMPANY IS RESPONDING TO A CLAIM FOR ADDITIONAL COMPENSATION OR TIME. APPROPRIATELY TAILORED. THIS TEMPLATE CAN BE USED TO ACCEPT OR REJECT THE CLAIM AND TO FOLLOW UP WITH THE APPROPRIATE CHANGE ORDER AND OTHER DOCUMENTATION IF ACCEPTED. NOTE THAT THE EXAMPLES WHICH FOLLOW ARE INTENDED TO PROVIDE A GENERAL, CONCEPTUAL APPROACH AND SHOULD NOT BE USED AS A VERBATIM TEXT. INDIVIDUAL LETTERS WILL NEED TO BE WRITTEN AND TAILORED TO THE SPECIFIC SITUATION GIVEN THE APPLICABLE FACTS AND CONTRACT TERMS.

Dear [*Name*]:

Please be advised that the Company is in receipt of your claim for [ADDITIONAL COMPENSATION / TIME/ OTHER].

Specifically, (*describe the nature of the claim*).

This claim has been reviewed and based on the facts and circumstances, together with the applicable terms and conditions of the above referenced Contract, the Company hereby[REJECTS / ACCEPTS] the claim as set forth herein. (*Where the claim is rejected, cite the applicable commercial terms and conditions governing the facts and circumstances raised by the claim*).

Example 1: Rejecting Claim for Additional Work - Your firm's obligation under the SOW / SOS included the [WORK / MATERIALS] which form the basis for your request for additional compensation. Under our Contract it was your firm's responsibility to [PERFORM / PROVIDE] the [WORK / MATERIALS] in question under the applicable SOW / SOS and Technical Specifications. Specifically, see (*cite reference, standard, or text as appropriate*). Accordingly, your request for additional compensation is denied.

Example 2: Rejecting Claim for Additional Time but no Additional Compensation - Your firm's obligations under the Contract was to [PERFORM / PROVIDE] the [WORK / MATERIALS] in accordance with the schedule and timelines set forth therein. Under the Contract the delays you request are not excusable. Please note that time of performance / delivery was, and remains, very important to the Company and was explicitly made "of the essence". Accordingly, the Company cannot grant your request for additional time and must insist on the original completion / delivery dates as agreed to by the parties. Your firm's failure to perform / provide the Work or Materials as required by the Contract would constitute a breach of your firm's obligations under our agreement with resulting damages to the Company. Please immediately confirm that your firm will adhere to the schedule as negotiated and agreed to by the parties

Example 3: Rejecting Claim for Additional Time and Compensation - Your firm's obligation under the Contract was to [PERFORM / PROVIDE] the

[WORK / MATERIALS] in accordance with the schedule and timelines set forth therein. Under the Contract the delays you request are neither excusable nor compensable. Please note that time of performance / delivery was, and remains, very important to the Company and was explicitly made "of the essence". Accordingly, the Company cannot grant your request for additional time and must insist on the original completion / delivery dates as agreed to by the parties. In addition, the parties specifically agreed that the Company would not be liable for delay claims. Your firm's failure to perform / provide the Work or Materials as required by the Contract would constitute a breach of your firm's obligations under our agreement with resulting damages to the Company. Please immediately confirm that your firm will adhere to the schedule as negotiated and agreed to by the parties.

Accordingly, the Company hereby denies your firm's claim.

The Company reserves all of its rights and remedies as provided in the Contract.

If you have any questions, please contact [*me*] at [*phone number and email address*].

Sincerely,

[*Name of Signatory*]   C: [*Project Director Name*]
[*Title of Signatory*]   [*Project Manager Name*]
                                              [*Other as appropriate*]

[*Attachment(s), if applicable*]

ATTACHMENT TO STEP 42 - CLOSEOUT CHECKLIST TEMPLATE

Contractor / Seller:	Description:	P.O. Number:	Date:

	Contract Close Out by Activity	Status	Date
1.	Project determines Contractor to be substantially completed		
2.	Project issues punch list items to Contractor		
3.	Contractor completes punch list items		
4.	Contractor completes all acceptance test / criteria		
5.	Project confirms removal of all equipment / temporary facilities		
6.	Construction / Engineering confirms acceptance of the work		
7.	Construction confirms return of Company equipment		
8.	Project confirms all spare parts are in place / available		
9.	Safety confirms return of badges		
10.	QA / QC receives all quality assurance / quality control documentation		
11.	Engineering receives as-built drawings and diagrams		
12.	Engineering confirms receipt of all necessary manuals / documents		
13.	Permitting receives permit compliance documentation		
14.	Permitting closes out all permitting compliance issues		
15.	Procurement receives all insurance certificate updates		
16.	Procurement facilitates final close out audit, if appropriate		
17.	Procurement resolves backcharges, claims and audit issues		

18.	Project Controls and Procurement calculate final Contract value		
19.	Project Controls and Procurement reconcile value in corporate system		
20.	Project Controls receives final invoice, affidavit and release		
21.	Accounts payable makes final payment / retention release		
22.	Return of letters of credit (if applicable)		
23.	Procurement forwards final Contract / PO documentation files to record retention and disposes of duplicates		
24.	Project Controls forwards invoices to records retention		
25.	Comments –		

Original Contract Amount: $	Final Contract Amount: $
Contract Start Date:	Contract Close Out Date:
Warranty Start Date:	Warranty End Date:
Contract Administrator / Procurement Analyst (Name / Signature / Date):	Contract Manager (Name / Signature / Date):

ATTACHMENT TO STEP 47 - LESSONS LEARNED

<u>Instructions for using this Desktop:</u>

Insert instructions specific to your organization's needs and requirements.

APPLYING A LESSONS LEARNED METHODOLOGY TO PROJECTS

Every good procurement professional understands that a big part of success is continual improvement by: (a) repeating successful behaviors and approaches and (b) learning from mistakes made in the past. This can only be achieved by having a disciplined "lessons learned" methodology as part of managing the procurement process.

LESSONS LEARNED DEFINED

"lessons learned" are born of useful projects or transaction-related information gained through experience. They provide a valuable technique or approach that you use to achieve a desired outcome to repeat or tailor to your procurement process. Conversely, a lesson learned can be by way of an undesirable result you wish to avoid in the future.

Ask questions to identify lessons learned… "What worked well or what didn't work so well?"

WHERE TO FIND LESSONS LEARNED

1. From an innovation or process improvement
2. From an adverse experience that is reduced to a process
3. From a positive experience that is reduced to a process

HOW TO USE LESSONS LEARNED

Lessons learned are used to improve the management of the procurement process.

A team approach to documenting and communicating improvements can help a company incorporate lessons learned into a process.

Your team needs to be a "learning organization" and cannot overlook its own experiences as a basis for improvement.

Do not assume that your collective experiences are passed along to the next person or group.

To be considered a learning organization companies must be proactive, capture lessons learned, and "cross-pollinate" the concepts. This is best achieved through documentation and training that exposes the information to others who may benefit from it.

Incorporating lessons learned into a process helps organizations operate with less risk, increased efficiency and more adaptability.

HOW TO DOCUMENT LESSONS LEARNED

Documenting useful lessons learned requires a clear understanding of the successes and/or failures of a project or transaction.

Because lessons learned serve as an important management tool in gaining organizational knowledge, managing risk, and improving performance, they must be relevant to future projects or transactions.

To build relevance into your "lessons learned" consider:

1. Identifying the circumstances in which the problem or positive development arose; and,

2. Defining the problem or positive development encountered, and providing concrete, practical solutions or recommendations based on this experience.

Statements such as "Clearly defined roles and responsibilities, along with a strong focus on communication channels, are essential to success" are not effective lessons learned. There is no context for such statements, and without context such statements are of little use.

While requiring more effort to develop, the examples in the following template make the same statement, but do so in a context that defines what management element is affected by the lessons learned, what the problem was that led to the lesson being learned, and how the lesson learned can serve future projects before a problem arises.

REQUIREMENTS FOR A LESSON LEARNED

In order to be easily accessible and beneficial across the Company, lessons learned should have the same look and content. Just as it is important that procurement professionals have a common understanding of the practices and terminology employed in their profession, it is equally important that the lessons learned they contribute be presented in a manner that is easily understood by their peers, successors and decision makers.

LESSONS LEARNED TEMPLATE

The template below contains a table and directions for recording lessons learned for your organization and for use by others:

LESSONS LEARNED TEMPLATE	
Department:	
Project Name:	
Point of Contact (POC): Name, phone, email.	
Which management areas are involved? (Integration, scope, time, cost, execution, project controls, quality, human resources, communications, risk, procurement.)	
Briefly describe the problem or situation including any relevant context such as stage of project.	
How was the problem resolved or the process improved?	
Lessons learned: How can this problem be avoided in the future or how can the process be improved?	

TEMPLATE INSTRUCTIONS

1. Identify the management area or areas in which the problem occurred or improvement was made.

2. The management areas listed below are common:
    <u>Scope</u>: the processes involved in ascertaining that the project includes all the work required.
    <u>Time</u>: the processes concerning the timely completion of the project or any of its components.
    <u>Cost</u>: the processes involved that assure the project is correctly estimated and completed within the budget.
    <u>Project Controls</u>: the process for reporting progress, schedule, cost and budget change control for the project
    <u>Quality</u>: the processes involved that assure the project will satisfy the objectives for which it was undertaken.
    <u>Human Resources</u>: the processes that select, train, organize and manage the project team.
    <u>Communications</u>: the processes concerning the timely and appropriate generation of reports and project information.
    <u>Risk</u>: the processes concerned with conducting risk management on the project.
    <u>Procurement</u>: the processes that purchase or acquire products and services.
    <u>Contract Management</u>: the processes and activities that integrate the various elements of management that are coordinated within the management groups to successfully achieve the objectives of the contract.

LESSONS LEARNED EXAMPLE EXPLAINED

1. Improvements may cut across more than one of the listed project management elements.

2. Include a brief description of the problem or process:

    a. This description should include all relevant information including the context. Context could include the project phase, nature of dispute, or type of redesign. To maintain uniformity among these descriptions it is preferable to use the common definition of project life cycle phases: initial phase (idea, charter, team formation), intermediate phase (project plan, baseline, progress acceptance), and final phase (approval, handover).

    b. The impact of the problem on project cost, schedule, and scope should also be considered and described.

3. The goal of "lessons learned" is to offer information that will be useful to managers in outside organizations in addition to managers within the organization under discussion. Therefore, descriptions should be written to be comprehensible to any project management professional. To achieve this result it is recommended that all descriptions should be free from insider organizational jargon. Acronyms should be spelled out.

4. How was the problem resolved?

    Provide a brief account of the steps that were taken to solve the problem or improve the process.

5. Other?

    The template should address any other areas of potential concern. For example, was the process circumvented by having suppliers or senior management negotiating terms or doing "back-door" deals that negatively affected the company's leverage or best interests? Was there reliance on letters of intent, memorandums of understanding or other preliminary agreements (or even the dreaded handshake-deals) that do not provide the protection of a well-articulated contract with a good scope of work? Were there excessive change orders indicating, perhaps, poor scope of work, inadequate planning, poor project management or other concerns? Was there appropriate "ownership" and commitment by the concerned individuals taking full responsibility for the success of the undertaking? Did the person(s) charged or involved with management the contract after it was signed fall into the trap of doing secret "side-bar" deals to mask what were really changes in scope, schedule, or cost?

Scope and contract language should also be reviewed for potential lessons learned. For example, was it clear that "as builts" would be provided as a prerequisite to final payment? Was the term "substantial completion", if used, properly defined as the point at which the purchaser was able to enjoy the beneficial use or occupancy of the project and could use and operate the project in all respects for its intended purpose? Was there a good order of precedence in the event of any inconsistency among the contract documents? Did the purchaser have unrestricted access to the project or work at all times for purposes of inspection or review?

Each project will be different and each self-critical analysis will have a unique set of facts and circumstances. Of course, it is important to capture what went "right" as well as what went "wrong".

EXAMPLE LESSONS LEARNED	
Department:	Department Name:
Project:	Project Name:
Point of Contact (POC): Name, phone, email.	[NAME], [PHONE], [EMAIL]
Which project management areas are involved? (Integration, scope, time, cost, execution, project controls, quality, human resources, communications, risk, procurement).	Cost Control
Briefly describe the problem or situation including any relevant context such as stage of project.	Company was overcharged by T&M Contractors and incorrect invoices were paid. Past practice of auditing at the end of the project proved problematic.
How was the problem resolved or the process improved?	An independent auditing firm was engaged and claims were made and settlement ultimately achieved at values below what could have been achieved if audit was performed earlier in the project.
Lessons learned: How can this problem be avoided in the future or how can the process be improved?	Conduct periodic (monthly, quarterly) mini-audits in addition to end of project audits.

CONCLUSION

Each organization should tailor the *PLAYBOOK* steps to fit its unique needs. *PLAYBOOK* is not the end result but a blueprint for the start of an organization's efforts to develop or amend its own playbook. Once those steps have been identified and finalized, the steps should be arranged in sequential order with associated descriptions, person(s) accountable and live links to the appropriate desktops, tools and resources.

As noted earlier, the real "art of the deal" is not doing the deal but "living with the deal". Many organizations fall into the trap of thinking the work of contracting is done when the contract is signed. It is not. The nature of language is such that no matter "how flat you make the pancake, there are always two sides." That being the case one could argue that there are "no facts…only interpretations". It would be the greatest mistake to simply assume that a contract is self-managing and can be "filed and forgotten". The only way to ensure that contracts are optimally managed from "cradle-to-grave" is to have a clear (and auditable) process - a Playbook - for doing so.

Made in the USA
San Bernardino, CA
11 March 2017